THE EMERGENCE OF THE SUPER-POWERS

A Short Comparative History of the U.S.A. and the U.S.S.R.

The Emergence of the Super-Powers

A SHORT COMPARATIVE HISTORY
OF THE U.S.A. AND THE U.S.S.R.

Paul Dukes
Lecturer in History, University of Aberdeen

HARPER COLOPHON BOOKS
Harper & Row, Publishers
New York and Evanston

This book was originally published by Macmillan and Co., Ltd., London in 1970.
It is here reprinted by arrangement.

THE EMERGENCE OF THE SUPER-POWERS: A SHORT COMPARATIVE HISTORY OF THE U.S.A.
AND THE U.S.S.R.

First HARPER COLOPHON edition published 1970 by Harper & Row Publishers, Inc.

LIBRARY OF CONGRESS CATALOG CARD NUMBER: 73-125353

to my
friends
in the U.S.A.
and the U.S.S.R.

Contents

Contents

Two empires will then share all the advantages of civilisation, of the power of genius, of letters, of arts, of arms and industry: Russia on the eastern side and America . . . on the western side, and we other peoples of the nucleus will be too degraded, too debased, to know otherwise than by a vague and stupid tradition what we have been.

BARON MELCHIOR VON GRIMM TO CATHERINE II
31 December 1790

Preface

Comparisons between the United States and the Soviet Union are made daily, yet there has never been much of an attempt to consider their historical development in a comparative manner. The idea of such an exercise has often been put forward, but its general amplification approached only by the German historian, E. Hölzle, and the Russo-American sociologist, P. A. Sorokin. The works of Hölzle, Sorokin and of others who have considered such particular aspects of the subject as mutual influences, cultural contacts and diplomatic exchanges are listed at the back of this book, which aims at synthesis rather than repetition.

One of the more judicious of the many examinations which have been made of the situation in which the super-powers have found themselves since the end of the Second World War, Vera Micheles Dean's *The United States and Russia* (Harvard U.P., 1947), commences with a preface which merits quotation at some length. Mrs Dean writes:

There can be few such soul-searching tasks as to attempt appraisal of a revolutionary epoch before the revolution has run its course – before its eddies, remote and near, have gradually disappeared, and the current of history runs smoothly again. *Questions of fact, of personal integrity, of moral judgment rise to plague one so bold as to write of nations astir with revolution and stirring others to inquiry into accepted ideas and values.*

Such questions become particularly harassing when relations between the United States and Russia are under discussion. To present Russia in too favorable a light is perhaps to lull the American people into a sense of security that events may prove to have been false. Yet to denounce Russia indiscriminately may be to mislead Americans into thinking that all movements for change in the world are Communist-inspired and therefore a threat to our institutions and way of life, and thus cause this country, the source in the past of so many bold and generous ideas, to become a bulwark of opposition to any alteration of the *status quo* abroad.

> *The best one can do under these trying circumstances is to take*
> *counsel of one's conscience, and to write about things as one sees*
> *them. Mistakes of fact or judgment can be dangerous. But far more*
> *dangerous is the temptation to interpret controversial events in*
> *such a way as to court this or that passing trend of public sentiment.*
> This is a time neither for fear nor complacency. Our main prob-
> lem is not whether we like Russia or dislike it, but whether,
> knowing what we do about it, we can find ways of living at peace
> with that country while continuing to adapt our own ideas and
> practices to the needs of a fast-changing age. Ralph Waldo
> Emerson described our task well when he wrote over a hundred
> years ago: 'If there is any period one would desire to be born in,
> is it not the age of Revolution; when the old and the new stand
> side by side and admit of being compared; when the energies of
> all men are searched by fear and hope; when the historic glories
> of the old can be compensated by the rich possibilities of the new
> era? This time, like all times, is a very good one, if we but know
> what to do with it.'

Although agreeing with most of what Mrs Dean says, particularly
with those remarks which I have italicised, I would like to make a
few comments on the above quotation. Firstly, the fact that she is
American inevitably makes her see the situation from the American
point of view. However, the substitution of just a few words would
make her remarks applicable to the Soviet situation. For example,
'to denounce America indiscriminately may be to lead Russians into
thinking that all movements for change in the world are capitalist-
inspired', or 'Our main problem is not whether we like America or
dislike it', and so on. Secondly, some observers would argue that, if
the present time is one of revolution, both the super-powers have
revealed themselves in recent years as anti-revolutionary reactionaries,
vainly attempting to maintain empires whose members yearn for
independence. While there is some superficial truth in such a view,
it is nevertheless fundamentally mistaken, I believe, for it attempts to
apply outdated concepts of previous revolutions to a new revolution
for which the terminology has still perhaps to be invented. In the
space age that we are now entering, Mrs Dean's observations and
those of Emerson are more, not less, relevant than they were in 1947.
  The basic argument of my book is that the emergence of the super-
powers has involved at least three hundred years of comparable
development, and that the historical examination of this process can
make a contribution to their mutual understanding and future

progress. Although the argument and the ideas relevant to it have been maturing for several years in various places, this book was mostly written in 1968 in the north-east of Scotland, where I was fortunate enough to find both an environment and sources of assistance favourable to its completion. Aberdeen and its hinterland have maintained close contact with both America and Russia during the period under discussion, and thus encourage an historical perspective on their present situation. At the University of Aberdeen many colleagues have encouraged my work, and made contributions to it of considerable importance. I should particularly like to express my thanks to John D. Hargreaves, who first suggested that a short book would be the best vehicle for my comparative study and then read the manuscript and made valuable comments on it; and Owen Dudley Edwards, now at the University of Edinburgh, who devoted many hours during his two years at Aberdeen to my diversion and instruction, and particularly to the improvement and extension of the points that the book attempts to put across. Edward Ranson carefully scrutinised the work from the American side, and Barry Hollingsworth, of the Russian Department at the University of Manchester, from the Russian. To them too I owe a great debt of gratitude. I am hardly less grateful to other senior and junior colleagues for the contributions that they have made to my project. To acknowledge these contributions in the manner they deserve would almost require a book devoted exclusively to them; here I can do no more than record their generosity in a general manner, and make clear that those to whom I am grateful include the staff of King's College Library, and senior and junior members of the History and other departments of the University at Old Aberdeen. Exceptional mention should perhaps be made of Myrtle Matthew, Walter N. Menzies and William Macdonald from the Library, and four former students of mine, Ronald Grant, Ian Stronach, James Tengey and Sara Dukes. Moyra Lees kindly typed most of the final draft of the book.

A few further points need to be made. Firstly, I have attempted to keep notes to a minimum, partly because the book is aimed at a public wider than that composed of people who thrive on them, partly because much of the information contained in it is sufficiently well known to those who would want documentation to make notes redundant. However, either the notes or the book list appended to the text name all the works from which I am conscious of having extracted data or ideas, and I have acknowledged the source of all recent authorities whom I have quoted, or from whom I have taken something which appears to be theirs rather than the common currency of historians dealing with the American and Russian fields. Most of the works referred to are in English, but this is because the book is addressed primarily to an English-reading public rather than because of a wilful bias towards them. Secondly, I have to admit that there are several areas of my subject to which I have given very little attention, in some cases hardly any at all: among these are the alienation of intellectuals, mutual commercial and cultural relations, religion, and the waste and conservation of natural resources. The main reason for this is ignorance and incompetence, which also account for the absence of tables and graphs. These inadequacies, as well as the shortcomings of what I have written, are exclusively my responsibility. Thirdly, by the time this preface is read, events may have occurred to change the perspective of the history of the super-powers, and to put my book somewhat out of focus. For example, domestic upheaval could strike either America or Russia, or each of them could radically alter its foreign policy regarding China or any other nation. In any foreseeable future, however, the under-standing between the U.S.A. and the U.S.S.R. which this book seeks to promote will not be superfluous, and, therefore, while its emphasis may be changed, the basis for their comparative history will not.

PAUL DUKES

King's College, Old Aberdeen
July 1969

1 Introduction: The Action, The Place, The Time

What is history? To most people vocationally connected with it, the study of the subject can best be defined briefly as hard work. Preparing or listening to lectures, reading or writing essays, assessing or undergoing assessment, the senior or junior historian rarely escapes an arduous routine. Such a daily process has its rewards, and by no means everybody engaged in it feels sunk beneath a stifling tedium. Equally, if we look upon the study of history as nothing more than a good liberal education, we are doing it a greater injustice than when we scorn the arduous preparation necessary for the basic competence to practise its deceptively simple arts. To put it more briefly, we must be able to walk before we can run, but should not walk all the time. In other words we are obliged as historians to consider now and again in a more profound manner the nature of the discipline as well as its external characteristics, to answer in a deeper sense the question, what is history? So are all those who take the subject seriously, whether professionally or not, and of whatever nationality.

Among the historians who have recently carried out this task, E. H. Carr, in his *What is History?*, has pointed out the principal reason for his colleagues' reluctance or inability to answer the great question during the last fifty years or so. In the nineteenth century, Carr argues, British historians tended to believe in historical progress because they thought that Great Britain was progressing. Since the First World War most of them have lost such belief because the country appears to have lost its momentum. The basic confidence of such men as Macaulay and Acton has been replaced by such pessimistic scepticism as that to be found in the following often quoted remarks from H. A. L. Fisher's preface to his *History of Europe*:

> Men wiser and more learned than I have discerned in history a plot, a rhythm, a predetermined pattern. These harmonies are concealed from me. I can only see one emergency following upon

another as wave follows upon wave, only one great fact with respect to which, since it is unique, there can be no generalisations, only one safe rule for the historian: that he should recognise in the development of human destinies the play of the contingent and the unforeseen.

Obviously we can see here that the loss of Great Britain's world primacy came as an overwhelming shock to members of a generation brought up to the belief that history had a plot, whose main thread was that God who had made Great Britain mighty would make her mightier yet. As wave upon wave of British troops had fallen in the war because their leaders could not foresee that the machine-gun and barbed wire had rendered such attacks suicidal, the history of the country did indeed lose its rhythms and its harmonies, and pomp and circumstance turned recessional.

When we turn to consider other historians in the world besides the British, we find many who still believe strongly in progress, who see clearly in history a predetermined pattern. Many are to be found in the two powers which have taken on Great Britain's world pre-eminence, the U.S.A. and the U.S.S.R. Let us take a glance at American and Soviet answers to aspects of the question, what is history? Historians in the younger of the super-powers present a more unanimous confidence, partly because they have to, partly because the future is likely to be brighter and greater for them than the present. An example of the way in which the past is seen by Soviet historians to have a progressive pattern can be taken from a dissertation concerned with the Pugachev Revolt of the 1770s and successfully defended in 1965. The author writes:

> To study peasant movements allows the working class and its party to know the struggle of its basic ally, to learn from the mistakes of this struggle. Through the study of the revolutionary traditions of the past is learned Soviet patriotism, love and pride for one's Fatherland.[1]

Even in the apparently unlikely field of the early Middle Ages in western Europe, a Soviet historian can find material relevant to contemporary problems. In an article published in 1967 he argues that, of the factors determining the necessity of studying any historical problem, the first and foremost should be the possibility of using the results of research for a better comprehension of the social problems of the present. Moreover, he continues:

The evolution of society and the changing demands of the class served by the historian necessarily alter the aspects of studying the past scientifically. Taking into consideration these ever-changing demands of the present and basing himself upon a constantly renewed system of methods and forms of cognition, the Marxist historian can and must incessantly reveal new sides of the phenomena of the past as the physicist is incessantly delving deeper and deeper into the mysteries of the structure of matter. A clear instance of this may be presented by studies of the west European early Middle Ages. Though the epoch has been studied for centuries, the number of scientific problems whose research may be of considerable social interest is very great.[2]

As examples, the author puts forward such problems as the history of towns, the interconnection of ethnic and political development, the evolution of human personality, the arts in the early Middle Ages, and the typology of early feudal societies. To turn to modern history and to take its most important event as far as the Soviet peoples are concerned, the October Revolution, historians in the U.S.S.R. look upon it as very much a vital issue of relevance to the problems of today. For them Lenin lives, and his analysis of the world's problems made half a century ago is still the best guide to present decision-making.

To a lesser degree, since it is more remote in time and less cataclysmic in its nature, the American Revolution has been looked upon by transatlantic historians as a far from dead issue. Clearly demonstrating their patriotism, American scholars have not until recently shown much interest in the loyalists, even though they were perhaps as numerous as the sympathisers with the national cause. The works of Charles A. Beard on the constitution and other subjects are unrestrained American Whiggery. In the preface to his *Age of Jackson*, Arthur M. Schlesinger Jr quotes F. D. Roosevelt and openly argues in the book that Jackson's administrations foreshadowed the New Deal. And yet, as Dr J. R. Pole reminds us in an article entitled 'The American Past: Is it Still Usable?',[3] the most extreme statement of the transatlantic instrumental view of history was probably made from the right wing by Conyers Read in his presidential address to the American Historical Association in 1949. To quote Dr Pole, who in turn quotes Read:

In a candid and unusual bid to qualify as the Zhdanov of the profession, Read disparaged both the work and the interests of those dedicated historians who take the past seriously for its own sake. 'It is the rare bird', he said, 'who is interested in the past simply as the past – a world remote, apart, complete. . . .' Read took the view that the liberal age, 'characterised by a plurality of aims and values', was a thing of the past, and that 'we must clearly assume a militant attitude if we are to survive'. This militant attitude involved the organisation of resources and the disciplined interpretation of history towards the propagation of American doctrines. 'This sounds', he added, 'like the advocacy of one form of social control as against another. In short, it is. But I see no alternative in a divided world.' His reassurance that his concept of control meant 'no menace to essential freedoms' could hardly have satisfied those whose views and interests might have run the risk of proving inessential.

However, the American would-be Zhdanovs, even at the height of McCarthyism, have never posed as great a threat to intellectual freedom in the U.S.A. as the real thing has constituted in the U.S.S.R. Moreover Dr Pole sees it as a healthy sign that in recent years a growing number of American historians have ignored Read's advice and tried to view the American past simply as the past. He welcomes the attempts to consider American Toryism and the complexities of the Jacksonian era. At the end of his article he writes :

Time, to come back to the beginning, is the element with which many American historians have had the greatest difficulty in coming to terms; yet they will see into the past, so far as it is given to us to do so, only when they recognise it, in its entirety, as the past. Time is not the enemy of the historian but it is not his friend; it is the prism, the only one, through which he may hope to perceive the dead.

But does Dr Pole thus completely destroy the case for instrumental history? In my view he does not. For if history is no more than a prism through which we hope to perceive the dead, many historians, even in tired old Great Britain, would want to have nothing more to do with it. By all means let those who wish to anatomise the corpse of the past do so. Let those who wish to study history for the glory of God do so. If a job in a school or university allows refugees to feel at home, outsiders to consider themselves in, if not quite the corridors of power, at least the common-rooms of respectability, may history flourish for these reasons too. The study of the subject allows many approaches to it. On the other hand, just as earlier British Whig[4] historians reflected and boosted the national self-confidence, a new generation of them could instil, is perhaps already instilling, a new confidence in the future of Great Britain in its post-imperial phase, as a part of a united Europe, a multiracial Commonwealth of fraternal equals, or some other supranational unit. Historians, ancient, medieval and modern, could widen the national focus without falling into rootless cosmopolitanism, for there is no reason why the history of Great Britain should not continue to play the central role to which it has become accustomed in British schools and universities.

However, there seems to me to be a strong case for another kind of Whig history, partly suggested by a consideration of views of history to be found currently in the super-powers. Are not historians in Great Britain in a particularly suitable position to contribute to the comparative historical study of the U.S.A. and the U.S.S.R., an instrumental exercise which could help increase their self-knowledge, reduce their mutual suspicion and assist their future progress by demonstrating that their histories show much greater similarity than either might now admit? For both the United States and the Soviet Union were born in revolution. Both have been profoundly influenced by their moving frontiers, by colonisation and immigration. The year 1812 gave a great boost to the national self-confidence in America and Russia. A decade or so later both achieved their full cultural independence of western Europe, and went on to produce a culture at least as vital as that produced by their former model. Slavery or serfdom was an unhappy feature of American and Russian life until the 1860s. These peculiar institutions were brought down by war, the Civil and the Crimean. The processes of industrialisation, although later in the Soviet case than in the American, brought comparable problems of social dislocation and alienation. Participation in the twentieth century's two world wars brought further vast changes to their domestic and even more to their international situation. Each still believes that it has a manifest destiny, a world mission, and that the other is the principal obstacle to its success.

Conceding that there might indeed be some surface similarity between the historical developments of the super-powers, a critic might nevertheless argue that to press this very far would be to distort historical reality, to force it into a preconceived mould. My reply to this would be that to carry out a historical task consciously brings far fewer pitfalls than to admit to no prejudice and to claim to be studying the past for its own sake. I think that it can be demonstrated that historians professing objectivity have neglected points of comparability between the developments of the U.S.A. and the U.S.S.R. By far the best way of making the case is to spell it out at some length, and this will be the main purpose of the rest of this book.

THE PLACE

If, as is often alleged, the twentieth-century struggle is indeed between godless Communism and Christian democracy, there can be no doubt that the Almighty weighted the scales in favour of his principal adherents and against his chief adversaries when he arranged the basic geographical conditions of the U.S.A. and the U.S.S.R. The only clear advantage possessed by the Soviet Union at the present time is size. Historically, this has often been a tremendous handicap; it has contributed as much as the poor climate and other drawbacks to the slow pace of Russian development. On the other hand, enemies such as Swedes, Poles, Frenchmen and Germans have found themselves swallowed up in the vastness of European Russia. Strategic thinkers such as Mackinder and his successors have seen the advantages of the domination of the Eurasian land mass, and, in the nuclear age, possession of one-sixth of the earth's surface may be much less of a liability than ever before. Three times as large as the United States, the Soviet Union may well find her size of increasing value in an era of super-powers. Geography, in other words, is no less evolutionary than history.

However, although subject to considerable fluctuations, the physical background is a relatively stable basis for a historio-geographical comparison; the stage for our drama does not alter to any great degree, although there are some changes in scenery. A helpful point of departure here is the observation made in 1955 by Dr Chauncy Harris:

that the Soviet Union and North America [i.e. including Canada and Mexico] are about equal in area (8½ million square miles) and in population (200 millions) and that in each an agricultural heartland abuts vast wastelands climatically unsuited to cultivation. In North America this heartland extends from the Atlantic seaboard westward to about the hundredth meridian and reaches from the Gulf of Mexico northward to the southern fringe of Canada. A corresponding agricultural heartland in the Soviet

Union, called the Fertile Triangle, stretches from corners at Leningrad on the Baltic Sea and Odessa on the Black Sea to somewhat east of the Ural Mountains.[5]

Developing this idea and looking first at the sea, we can see that although Russia's coastline is very long, much of it is north of the Arctic Circle and not yet of any great use. One of her historic drives has been to ports open at least part of the year, firstly to the Baltic Sea, then to the Black Sea and finally to the Pacific Ocean. North America has been better endowed with exploitable coastline, although a considerable amount of it there too is frozen for most of the year. Except in the case of Alaska, however, the United States has not been significantly troubled by the ice problem on her external waters and has continued use of the Atlantic Ocean, the Gulf of Mexico and the Pacific Ocean. While the sea has been more agreeably arranged for the U.S.A. than for Russia, a broad comparison can be made between their manner of exploitation of the Atlantic Ocean and the Baltic Sea, the Gulf of Mexico and the Black Sea, and the eastern and western littorals of the Pacific Ocean. In the eighteenth century St Petersburg and other towns on the Baltic, forming the window on the west, maintained Russia's connection with the European civilisation that stretched over the Atlantic to Boston and other ports in the American wilderness. America's takeover of *her* Mediterranean, the Gulf of Mexico, in two principal stages during the first half of the nineteenth century might be likened to Russia's assimilation of the northern and eastern shores of the Black Sea, her outlet to *the* Mediterranean, a few years before. The Crimea and the northern shore of the Black Sea are juxtaposed here to the Louisiana Territory, and the Caucasus to Texas. Cosmopolitan Odessa, a centre for agricultural exports, may equate to New Orleans in the nineteenth century, and Batumi, an outlet for oil, to Galveston in the twentieth. Continuing this over-fanciful comparison and quickly passing over a surface similarity between Russia's Central Asia, where nomadic tribesmen were subdued in the late nineteenth century, and America's Far West, where the Red Indians made their last stand at about the same time, we come to the two Pacific shores face to face. Vladivostok, although founded in 1860, had some years to go before it could begin to rival San Francisco, however, and not even the most fervent supporter of the Soviet Union could yet call its Far East a Siberian California.

Leaving the seas, we move inland along the rivers, which have played an equally vital part in the history of the super-powers. Kievan Russia grew up on the Dnieper, and was infiltrated by Northmen coming up the Western Dvina and other rivers, just as they penetrated America along the St Lawrence. With the growth of Muscovy, the rivers rising in the Valdai Hills to the west of Moscow were vital arteries for the new society. They included not only the Dnieper and Western Dvina, but also the Don and the Volga and its tributaries. Outstanding among these became the Volga, whose value would have been even greater had it flowed into the Black Sea rather than into the landlocked Caspian. The U.S.A.'s nearest equivalent to the Volga, the Mississippi–Missouri, did not become very important until the nineteenth century. Before this, the rivers leading into the hinterland from the conveniently indented eastern seaboard, the James, the Hudson, the Delaware and others, were of most service. The rivers remote from the first centres of civilisation assisted exploration and communication, whether through Siberia along the Ob, Yenisei and Lena, into Central Asia along the Syr Darya and Amu Darya, across to the Russian Pacific along the Amur, or down to the American south-west along the Rio Grande and Colorado, up to the north-west along the Columbia, from northern to southern California along the Sacramento and San Joaquin. While the heartland rivers were supplemented by canals, those beyond it were not, partly because this would have been less useful in their case, more because their exploitation was not fully developed before the arrival of the railroad and, in some cases even the aeroplane.

Stepping ashore, we should return to the question of the super two's heartlands. As Professor Harris points out, the Soviet Union's is smaller than N. America's 386 million acres under cultivation in 1952 as opposed to 440 million. The average Russian crop yields, moreover, have always failed to reach the American level. This has no doubt been partly due to the human factor, but two basic physical features appear to have been more influential. Firstly, a large part of the Soviet Union is within the Arctic Circle; in the U.S.A. this applies only to part of the state of Alaska. Both Leningrad and Moscow are in a latitude north of Ketchikan, Alaska. Vladivostok, the most southerly point of the eastern U.S.S.R., is further to the north than Boston, which lies approximately in the same latitude as Tashkent in Central Asia and Tiflis in Transcaucasia. Nearly two-thirds of the Soviet Union is covered by northern forest and desolate tundra; of the U.S.A., except again for Alaska, none. Secondly, the vast flattened and distorted rhomboid shape of the U.S.S.R. (as opposed to the irregular triangle that is North America) has given it a continentality of climate that increases in extremity towards the east and makes it virtually impossible to farm in deeper Siberia. Cold is an enemy there to the north, dryness to the south, where in the effort to extend the area under cultivation, Professor Harris tells us, 'Much land now tilled is as poor as the abandoned farmland of the Appalachian Mountains or the Dust Bowl in the United States'. There is no Soviet equivalent to the rich American Corn Belt and Cotton Belt. Professor Harris explains:

> The Fertile Triangle, the agricultural heartland, has a cool continental semi-arid climate similar to that of the spring-wheat region of the Prairie Provinces of Canada and the Dakotas of the United States. These areas are characterized by relatively low crop yields per acre, high variability of yields from year to year, a severely restricted range of crops, and little possibility of increasing yields through more intensive farming. Odessa, on the warm southern margin of the Triangle, is as far north as Duluth, Minnesota. Actually, its summer temperatures are somewhat higher than those of Duluth, being more nearly those of Omaha, Nebraska. But its annual precipitation is about ten inches less than either Duluth or Omaha. Because of the short growing season and the relatively meager and irregular rainfall, farming in the Fertile Triangle, as in the American spring-wheat region, is heavily dominated by grains, mainly wheat, rye, and oats. The richest soils of the Soviet Union, the fertile chernozems (blackearth), stretch in a broad sweeping band along the semi-arid southeastern edge of the Triangle, but their productivity is hampered by the scanty and uncertain rainfall.

The parts historically played within the agricultural heartlands of the steppe and the prairie, the Russian and American forests, have been central to the drama. Carving and burning out small plots of land in the wooded regions, or farming more extensively but with irrigation and construction problems in the rolling plains, the frontiersman in both societies has struggled against vast natural problems in an epic manner. One difference between the histories of the super two as yet unmentioned, however, is the relatively minor significance of mountains during the expansion of Russia. The Urals are in many cases no more than high hills and the Caucasus does not come on the scene significantly until the nineteenth century. Even today the mountains of Central Asia and eastern Siberia are still on the fringe of the life of the Soviet Union. In America, on the other hand, the Appalachians were important moulding influences from the middle of the eighteenth century for at least another hundred years, and the crossing of the Rocky Mountain barrier was one of the most momentous episodes in the great trek west.

Turning from the land, we look finally at the comparative question of natural resources, and put ourselves again in the expert hands of Professor Harris, who informs us that the fuel and water power constituting the total energy resources of the Soviet Union have been calculated to be 23 per cent of the world's total as compared with the U.S.A.'s 29 per cent. While the U.S.A.'s resources are for the most part conveniently located, however, 90 per cent of the U.S.S.R.'s are in sparsely populated Soviet Asia. Similarly, although by no means short of metals and other raw materials necessary for an industrialised economy, the Soviet Union does not have them as readily accessible as they are in the United States. The Soviet predicament is well described by Professor Harris, who writes :

The enormous size of the Soviet Union creates special problems for heavy industry. Many parts of the country are far from cheap sea transport and therefore even bulky commodities must be transported over vast distances by relatively expensive overland hauls. One measure of the energy needed to overcome the space friction involved in operating the Soviet economy is the consumption of fuel in transportation. It is estimated that Soviet railroads require about 30 per cent of all coal produced. Smaller countries of Western Europe, such as the United Kingdom and Germany, use only a third as high a proportion of their coal in railroad transport.

One way in which the government is attempting to solve the distance problem and to economize on transportation is by encouraging as much regional self-sufficiency as possible. Thus the government has called for the development of local sources of raw materials near existing markets, of food production in industrial districts, and of manufacturing in agricultural areas. The growing of wheat in the central industrial district and the development of cotton textile factories in Central Asia are cases in point.

The total physical resources of energy and metalliferous ores in the Soviet Union appear to be sufficient for several further decades of further expansion in heavy industry. But the cost of utilizing these resources is another matter ! The real costs of producing coal and iron ore, for example, appear to be rising as the high-quality, easily mined, and accessible deposits become depleted and less favorable ones must be used. It is well to remember, however, that in no other country in the world has so high a proportion of the total national income been poured into the development of heavy industry, and to judge by past experience, one may predict that the government will be willing to pay the high price necessary for its continued growth.

'Past experience' in the Soviet case goes back to the middle of the seventeenth century, when Russian heavy industry was founded at the armaments works at Tula. In both Russia and America at this time, attitudes to economic problems as well as to others were forming in a manner recognisable at a much later time in the history of the super-powers. It is to the fourth dimension, which is fundamental to the argument of this book, that we must now address ourselves.

THE TIME

Many of us grew up to the idea that modern Western history dawns at about the end of the fifteenth century. At Oxford and Cambridge modern history still begins, for some purposes at least, with the fall of Rome. The choice for most historians today would probably be somewhere near the middle of the seventeenth century, although a strong case can be made for placing the great dividing line in the eighteenth or the nineteenth century. It all depends on where the emphasis is placed: if on the growth of learning and humanism, the late fifteenth century can be chosen; if on the separation between the classical era and what followed, the fall of Rome; if on the demographic and industrial revolutions, either the eighteenth century when these two great developments appear to leave the ground, or the nineteenth when they rise to a great height.

The reasons for the choice of the middle of the seventeenth century, which is made here for additional reasons appropriate to the main theme of the book, are basically as follows. Firstly, the origins of modern capitalism have been placed in this period. Secondly, a crisis throughout Europe at the time acted as the birth-pangs of modern government. Thirdly, the end of the Thirty Years War in 1648 meant the conclusion, militarily and diplomatically, of the first clearly discernible phase in the modern struggle for Europe. Fourthly, the great changes in scientific thinking which occurred in the seventeenth century have been widely looked upon as the foundations of that rationalism which led on to the Enlightenment and modern intellectual life.

How do the future super-powers, at this time peripheral appendages of Europe, fit into the pattern just outlined, if at all? To answer the question briefly and to take first the economic aspect of the problem, the subject of considerable controversy when concerned with western Europe, we have the authoritative view of Lenin that economic unity must precede political unity, and that such an indication of the formation of a modern state at the eastern end of Europe must primarily be sought in the growth of an all-Russian market. Wisely, since not much research on the subject had been done at the time he was writing, Lenin placed the development of this market 'approximately since the seventeenth century'. The evidence produced by Soviet historians to support Lenin's assertion has been necessarily fragmentary and their arguments have therefore been inconclusive. Nevertheless qualified support can be given to the contention that Russia was becoming a more cohesive economic unit, or collection of units, by the middle of the seventeenth century. This trend was encouraged by commercial ties with western Europe, particularly England, to which Russia sent furs and naval stores.

While the seventeenth century was one long crisis for the early Romanovs, Russia did conform to some extent to the political pattern detectable in other parts of the continent at the middle of the century. Urban disturbances revealed a profound malaise, to which a response was the Code of 1649, an attempt to give Muscovite society greater definition, and thus a higher degree of stability. To give the Code the widest possible sanction, the Tsar summoned the *zemskii sobor*, or national assembly, but was soon to dispense with it. Although threatened by other revolts in the cities and in the provinces, the largest of which was that of Stenka Razin, the Romanov dynasty emerged from the mid-century crisis on a firmer foundation than was discernible when Michael Romanov was placed on the throne in 1613. The decline of the Boyar Duma and the system of appointment to government posts known as *mestnichestvo* showed that the medieval organisation of the governing class was giving way to a new military-bureaucratic establishment of which the autocrat would continue to be the keystone. The assimilation of the Ukraine in the period following the termination of the Thirty Years War both reflected and increased the greater hold that the Romanovs were gaining over the nascent Russian Empire.

Culturally, too, Europe's eastern frontier entered the modern world in the 1650s with the reform of the Orthodox Church. Changes in Western Christianity had percolated to the frontier through Poland and the Ukraine, and produced a tremendous upheaval in Holy Russia leading to a schism. The Old Believers henceforth dropped out of Muscovy as much as they could, while the members of the reformed church were ready for the continuation of the modernisation of the Empire by Peter the Great.

Across the Atlantic on the other frontier, the shock wave of Europe's crisis was distinctly felt. Preoccupied by events at home and then most interested in the West Indies, England allowed the North American colonies to experience two decades or so of 'salutary neglect'. Forced to look after themselves, the colonies worked to develop economic prosperity. The extent to which they succeeded was reflected in the attempt of the restored monarchy to incorporate them much more comprehensively than before in the framework of England's economy. While the focus of attention was still on the West Indies, tobacco and, later, furs and naval stores were considered items worthy of exclusive export from North America to the mother country, and the colonies were increasingly looked upon as a useful market for English goods.

Left to themselves from 1640 to 1660, the colonies also strengthened their local governments, felt the early intimations of independence, and took the first steps towards federation, in the northern group at least, with the formation of the 'United Colonies of New-England' in 1643. Joined together mainly for purposes of mutual defence against the French, the Dutch and the Indians, these settlements thus demonstrated both their extension of old European rivalries and their concern with new threats from the frontier.

Self-reliant though they may have been politically, the North American colonies were still at mid-century dependent on the mother country from the cultural point of view. A certain plainness of style was encouraged by the new environment, and the extravagances of the Restoration were difficult to reproduce across the Atlantic. This, however, may be another way of saying that colonial creativity was still a pale reflection of British and European models.

Four general observations have so far been made about the future super-powers around the years 1640 to 1660. Firstly, both Russia and America were entering the early stages of capitalist development, and benefited from their connections with the European economy, particularly the English, soon to become the first in the world to undergo industrial revolution. Secondly, the pattern of much of the political future was already emerging in, for example, the heavily centralised emphasis of Russian government and the embryonic federalism of American. Thirdly, wars in central and western Europe meant considerable repercussions to the east of the continent and across the ocean. Fourthly, the frontier nature of their situation rendered the precursors of the super two incapable of doing much else besides following the cultural lead of more settled societies.

For the next century or so of American and Russian history these four observations continue to be applicable. Let us briefly see how this is so, bearing in mind that the focus of attention is not yet as close as it will become in the second chapter and that the present examination is extremely cursory. Again to look firstly at the economy, Europe's steppe and transatlantic frontiers expanded their activity considerably from 1660 to 1760. Russia and America were still useful, even indispensable, to Europe, particularly Great Britain, as suppliers of furs and naval stores, and increasingly afforded market opportunities. The subordination of the North American colonies to the mother country, however, meant that their industrial development was discouraged (although northeastern commerce boomed), whereas in Russia, as mercantilist as other powers, all possible encouragement was given to domestic manufacturers and industrialists. The great leap forward in the economy associated with Peter the Great was anticipated in the reigns of his predecessors and continued under his successors. Serfdom, which was more firmly clamped down by Peter, acted as a brake on progress not only in the industrial but also in the commercial and agricultural spheres. While it is certainly correct to say that there were by 1760 farmers producing for markets which stretched throughout the Empire and beyond, there were still great pockets of a closed subsistence economy. Primitive ploughs and the strip system were still the norm over a large area. Russian society reflected this backwardness; the peasantry accounted for over 90 per cent of the population of central Russia. Of course there were different types of peasant: those belonging to the state and those belonging to the noble and ecclesiastical landlords; the rich and the poor; the submissive and the rebellious. Quite a few worked at least part of the year in towns or manufacturing enterprises. Some ran away to join the Cossacks in the steppe or the Poles across the border. In other words there was much more variety and mobility among the peasantry in Russia than gloomy pictures of a solid mass of suppressed serfs often suggest. The town population was comparatively small, as was the number of those in the clerical ranks. The landed nobility was a tiny class, but all-powerful; the greatest landlord of them all was, of course, the autocrat, who was at once their patron and their creature. In America, although there too the subsistence economy was by no means unknown, prosperity was easier come by and social relationships were freer from the first, at least for the whites. Some of them worked their passage through the indentured servant system, but once their time was up they could seek their fortunes in the nascent towns or on the frontier with no more restraint than their initial poverty. This did not mean the absence of social tension – rather the reverse. A tidewater–frontier split, which was also a division between the establishment and the under-privileged, was apparent in many colonies from north to south and threatened to tear some of them apart before independence. Pressures of this nature were to some extent resolved in the plantation colonies, of course, by the mass importation of Negro slaves.

In government, centralisation remained the predominant Russian theme while the American colonies took some further steps towards a federal organisation at the same time as conducting separate administrations usually more connected to the mother country than to each other. Again, in the Russian case the reign of Peter the Great is extremely significant, with its introduction of the senate, colleges, procurator-general and other new officials and bodies, but it is also necessary to see Peter's work as a very important stage in the more general evolution of a military–bureaucratic absolutism supported by an all-powerful nobility. The concentration of all power at the centre was more the expression of a wish than a description of reality. Local governors often behaved in an independent and illegal manner; many of the Tsar's subjects ran away to the rough democracy of the frontier. The army was as much used to keep some measure of control at home as to fight against foreigners. Meanwhile the American colonies governed themselves to a large extent in fact at the same time as being officially subject to king, Parliament and a bewildering number of agencies of one kind and another. Their support for the series of wars for empire fought between Britain and her European rivals, principally France, was half-hearted, although George Washington and others were to gain some useful experience fighting both Indians and white men. On the whole Europe was becoming remote, but colonial governments suffered from land distance at the same time as benefiting from sea distance. Colonies such as Virginia and

Pennsylvania stretched way to the west, and intrepid individuals were already crossing the mountains. Tidewater administrations were finding it difficult to hold sway over frontier settlements. Under pressure from Great Britain and the threat of war, the centrifugal nature of American politics was combated in 1754 by the Albany Plan of Union. But this came to nothing, and the degree of co-operation by the colonies among themselves or with the mother country was very small during the Seven Years War.

In the cultural sphere the age of reason and enlightenment reached out across the Atlantic and the European continent. Both American and Russian outlooks were still basically religious, but new elements of secular rationalism had infiltrated quite noticeably by 1760. Reaction to this innovation reflected divisions in society as well as the church; this is as true of the Great Awakening in America as of the schism in Russia, in both of which movements the lower social depths tended to adhere to the old-time religion. The frontier cultures were still largely ancillary to that of the western European metropolis, but by 1760 could produce men of such stature as Benjamin Franklin and Michael Lomonosov, of whom more below. Literacy rates would be higher in America than Russia at this time, but the majority of people in both regions would be unconscious of the principal intellectual movements of the time and not very much affected by them.

Russian culture was old, and American new. The Slavs in Kiev were not more barbaric than many other races in Europe, and their reception of Christianity in 900 meant closer connections with the rest of Europe. Such links were strengthened by the arrival of the Northmen, who, apart from the Indians, were the first to establish tenuous connections between the future super-powers. Muscovy's ties with Byzantium rather than Rome tended to separate eastern from western European medieval culture, it is true, but the split was never complete and, in the world context, the great schism was but a parochial difficulty. If Russia appears backward and remote at the dawn of the modern age, this was because of her frontier situation, the shocks that she had withstood from the Mongols and others sweeping across from Asia. Western Europe was able to move ahead, to develop relatively sophisticated systems of business and class, law and government, art and thought, because it was operating in conditions of comparative peace, protected from Genghis Khan and his successors by the longsuffering Russians.

The frontier was not the place for the refinements of the drawing-room. This was as true for the New World as for the Old. European ideas and procedures were simplified or caricatured in the wilderness, and some of them completely jettisoned. Yet many of the early emigrants to America were literate, even academic theologians, and even the most ignorant of them was in some sense a bearer of Western culture, centuries ahead in know-how of the indigenous inhabitants, who were ignorant of the firearm or even the wheel. American colonial culture was a direct offshoot of the most advanced that the world could provide in the seventeenth and eighteenth centuries. This gave it a strong initial advantage over the Russian, which struggled to throw off the dead weight of a long and sad past, while the colonies experienced at least something of a youthful exuberance.

Already by 1760, then, many of the features of the U.S.A. were formed or in process of formation, although the American Revolution had not yet occurred. To a lesser extent, but clearly enough, the same can be seen to have been so of the U.S.S.R., even though another century and a half were to elapse before its creation.

2 The Age of the Democratic Revolution, 1763–1815

In 1763 the great conflict of the mid-eighteenth century came to an end. Known commonly to Europeans as the Seven Years War and to North Americans as the French and Indian Wars, it varied from continent to continent in significance as well as name. For Russia the war meant further emergence on to the European stage, as her troops entered Berlin; for the colonies it brought the removal of the French threat from Canada, after Wolfe had defeated Montcalm near Quebec. Now the Americans were less ready than ever to be an integral part of the imperial administration and to contribute to its upkeep, at the same time that the British Government decided to exert firmer financial and other forms of control over the Empire. The result of the inevitable clash was the War of Independence, or American Revolution. The shock waves of this colonial breakaway crossed the Atlantic to make a contribution of some importance to the even more influential French Revolution. The combined impact on the rest of the world of the two great upsets has been well described by Professor R. R. Palmer in *The Age of the Democratic Revolution*,[1] from which book this chapter steals its title. Professor Palmer, however, underestimates the degree of imperial Russia's participation in the world-wide movement for the recognition of the rights of man. To the east as well as to the west of the main cockpit, the demand for liberty and equality was loud and persistent towards the end of the eighteenth century, and both the new regime in the United States and the old in Russia feared for their survival. At the end of the era of the democratic revolution, which is extended here to 1815, however, both countries had cause for renewed and increased confidence. By 1815 the Russians had defeated Napoleon and marched through the streets of Paris. The 'Marseillaise' gave way, as in Tchaikovsky's celebratory overture, to 'God Save the Tsar'. The Americans had inflicted reverses on the British on sea and land, and, while making a brief 'tactical withdrawal' from Washington, had soon driven the invaders back from Baltimore. During this spirited counter-attack the rockets' red glare, the bombs bursting in the air, had given proof through the night to Francis Scott Key and his fellow Americans that their flag was still there. In just over fifty years, then, both America and Russia had moved from a position of relative obscurity to one of considerable prominence. Already in 1777 the American diplomat Silas Deane had forecast that Great Britain, the United States and Russia would dominate the world. 'Russia like America is a new state', he observed, 'and rises with the most astonishing rapidity.'[2] In 1790 her correspondent Baron Melchior von Grimm had written to Catherine that America and Russia would soon be so powerful that Europe would be crushed between them.[3] By 1815 Napoleon and many other Europeans would be ready to agree with Deane and Grimm.

Both America and Russia experienced important political development as well as growing international influence during the years between 1760 and 1815, and the domestic picture may be conveniently considered before a closer look can be taken at the foreign. At the beginning of the period both the British and Russian imperial administrations continued to muddle along, making some attempts at reform, but without much success. A common insuperable barrier remained distance, of course; the Atlantic took weeks to cross, as did the Great Russian plain; frontiers were far off. Administrative decision could not be adapted to the time-lag necessary for execution; information assisting such decision was always out of date and often garbled. The British predicament was compounded by the increasing sense of alienation demonstrated by the colonists, from government if not yet from king and country. The Russian peasants felt little attachment to a governing class under German and French cultural domination. The failure of reform in both cases led to great violent crises in the 1770s.

The American colonists, to take them first, had long suffered incoherence and inconsistency from the authority placed over them, the imperial administration just growing in a topsy-turvy manner out of that of the kingdom and subject to the whims and upsets of the political world of ins and outs, a toy in the patronage game. From 1763 to 1774 some ministers, for example Shelburne and Chatham, tried to bring order out of chaos; others, such as Townshend and to a lesser extent Grenville, more than succeeded in firmly putting it back there. The colonies, not yet ready for unity with British co-operation, as the failure of the Albany Plan of Union had shown in

1754, more closely approached it under the pressure of British intransigence. The notorious Stamp Act led to the first Congress, the Coercive Acts to the Continental. The die was cast, and the first shot all but fired. A sufficient number of colonists, who could not agree how to worship God, organise their government or expand their frontier, resolved to fight together for what they believed to be their rights, for freedom.

George Washington had to be a great man, whether or not he wanted to be one, whether or not, indeed, he had the necessary qualifications. Of course his greatness was to a large extent thrust upon him after his death, while much of his human frailty was interred with his bones. Never like Lenin placed in a mausoleum, Washington was to occupy a place in the hearts of Americans in the nineteenth century no less great than Lenin in the hearts of Soviet citizens soon after the October 1917 Revolution. For the moment let it be enough to say that Washington, a jack of many trades, was also master of one, giving a sufficiently strong impression of probity and perseverance to persuade the famous four thousand to winter with him at Valley Forge, in a word, to be that indispensable attribute of revolution, its figurehead. Washington must not be debunked any more than apotheosised, admittedly, and his leadership was certainly pragmatic, determined and courageous. Even a brief study of contemporary American sources reveals that he has gained enchantment with the passage of time, however. So has independence. United in war, or too preoccupied to notice their disunity, the revolutionaries realised when peace came that not only did they hate British government in particular, but that they had no great affection for government in general. Somehow, unexpectedly, to form a new contract appeared as difficult as to break the old one.

About three months before the outbreak of the War of Independence in America, a great emancipationist peasant war had come to an end in Russia with the execution in Moscow of its leader, Emelian Pugachev. Pugachev had claimed to be Peter III, who had been murdered in the coup which had brought his none too reluctant widow, Catherine II, more commonly known as the Great, to the throne. The impersonation was difficult for Pugachev, an illiterate Don Cossack, to carry off, and was seen through by many of his lieutenants. It was necessary, all the same, to give the revolt legitimacy at a time when the doctrines of popular sovereignty had not been consciously realised by the Russian people. Pugachev first raised his hastily manufactured standard at the river Yaik in September 1773, and was handed over by some treacherous supporters to the government troops near the same region a year later, having described a large destructive circle through the Ural industrial region to the town of Kazan and then back down the river Volga. Although Pugachev never got near to Moscow, he unleashed anti-government feeling there and in St Petersburg, and gained sufficient support from Cossacks, nomadic tribesmen and peasants to give detachments of regular soldiers a real run for their money, and to make Catherine fear for her own security.

The extent of her alarm was revealed in the savage thoroughness of the revolt's suppression. Catherine also tried to erase the name of Pugachev from the mind of the masses by such steps as changing the name of the river Yaik to Ural, moving his native village to the opposite bank of the Don and renaming it too. She appears to have made some attempt as well at alleviating the economic predicament that had contributed so much to Pugachev's emergence. But there was much more eradication by force than amelioration through reform, and the law on the administration of the provinces of 1775, to a considerable degree prompted by the peasant war, falls more into the first than the second category. This law attempted to increase the government's control over the Empire by, among other means, allowing an elective noble element to dominate the lower levels of provincial administration. The nobles themselves had asked for something like this at the unsuccessful Legislative Commission of 1767, and Catherine had been assiduously studying Blackstone in French translation and thinking of creating a Russian gentry to act as J.P.s. Her earlier mentor, Montesquieu, had inculcated in her the idea of the separation of powers, and this too she attempted to incorporate in the reform. She did not share Montesquieu's view of an independent nobility, but at the same time her establishment was composed of the top ranks of that class and dominated the lower ranks of the nobility, who were now to be given new service in local government. Precipitated as it was by Pugachev and russified by powerful tradition, the new arrangement of 1775 meant in the end not much more than the increased bureaucratisation and reinforcement of the alliance between autocracy and nobility that held the state together throughout the eighteenth century.

This alliance was yet further strengthened in 1785 with the Charter of the Nobility, guaranteeing important corporate and individual rights to the second estate. The Charter of the Towns of the same date, and a charter for the state peasants, which was never promulgated, were to take care of the third estate, the serfs of the nobles still being considered as having no independent legal existence. Thus the socio-political structure of the Russian Empire would be completed in such a manner that each class would have a definite part assigned to it under the autocrat, and the Empire become a well-integrated, smoothly functioning machine. But such a rationalisation was of course impossible to achieve.

Some educated Americans became keen at this time to pursue a similar order, although in the structure of government rather than society. Since independence had been achieved, the states had largely gone their separate ways and the central government suffered a very precarious existence, finding it particularly difficult to carry conviction in its dealings with other nations. But such an unsatisfactory state of affairs might not have become critical if it had not been for the renewed outbreak of violence. This time it took the form of Shays' Rebellion, a debtor movement confined to Massachusetts, but of wider incendiary potential to Washington, who was prompted to write 'There are combustibles in every State which a spark might set fire to'. And so the leaders of society came together to put limits on the freedom for which they had fought, soon forgetting that they had no right to do so.

The federal constitution produced at long last the form of government that might have been brought in more than thirty years before if the Albany Plan of Union had been successful, except that now the colonies were states and the central administration American rather than British. Powers were separated and balanced, partly because Montesquieu and his like had said that they ought to be so, to a greater extent because local adaptation of British tradition had made necessary such an arrangement. If this had not been the case, the constitution would have remained a scrap of paper, as did so many of the fine schemes for political reform put forward in Tsarist Russia. Even as things were, it was still no more than a scrap of paper until Washington and his entourage had put words into deeds and read between the lines to find some of the words.

Washington had been a competent estate manager, a dogged revolutionary leader, and now turned out to be a judicious president. He was at first reluctant to play the part that his enthusiastic fellow-countrymen assigned him, and this reluctance was well justified before his retirement, as their enthusiasm changed to execration. Washington helped produce a strong and solvent central administration from virtually nothing, for which he was considered tyrannical, kept his young country out of what could have been a crippling war, for which he was vilified, and then gave a farewell address full of good advice, which hardly anybody listened to.

Among his recommendations for the development of the federal union, Washington adjured Americans to avoid the 'baneful effects of the spirit of party'. The 1796 election to choose his successor, for which the farewell address was a campaign speech at the same time as being a valedictory *tour d'horizon*, was in fact the first to show clear signs of such spirit. The influence of party was by no means entirely baneful; indeed, it contributed much to the vitality of political life as two principal groups formed on ideological foundations suggested by Hamilton and Jefferson. Like their heirs, the Republicans and the Democrats of today, however, the first two parties had more in common than they would usually have admitted. Both leaders were in favour of the constitution, although Jefferson wanted it interpreted more strictly than Hamilton, until he became president at least. Both were in favour of a limited suffrage, although Hamilton admired the European class system and feared 'mobocracy' more than Jefferson, who wanted more people to get the vote as they became educated, and the eventual development of an American popular sovereignty. For all this large area of basic agreement, party strife reached a hysterical pitch as news of the radical developments in the French Revolution spread to the New World. The in-party, the Federalists, denounced and to some extent persecuted Jefferson's more liberal supporters. Jefferson's victory in the election of 1800 was feared by some to be the end of all rectitude and stability in government. It soon turned out to be nothing of the kind; in any case it was stopped from going off the rails by John Marshall, a Federalist in the impartial guise of Chief Justice. However, as troubles stemming from the Napoleonic wars increasingly engaged Jefferson's attention, and his successor, Madison, found himself at war with Great Britain because of them, party strife was far from forgotten.

In Russia the outbreak of the French revolutionary wars transformed an already ageing conservative Catherine II into an old reactionary. Any further projects for internal reform that she may have been contemplating were abandoned, and she probably counted herself lucky to die a peaceful death as the cry for liberty and equality went up in Russia as well as in other European countries. The reign of Catherine's son Paul, like that of her husband, Peter III, came to an early abrupt end as Paul, like Peter, incurred the wrath of the nobility and brought a palace revolution on himself. Before he was murdered Paul was able to show the way to many of the reforms of the nineteenth century, although much of his work was immediately undone by his son, Alexander I. For example, a decree was passed making the crown the hereditary property of the Romanovs and defining the order of succession. Alexander infringed this definition, of course, by assenting to the coup that gave him the throne, and probably by conniving at the death of his father too.

Alexander had been educated to be a rational and progressive monarch; he was also a man of great charm and, in spite of the manner of his arrival on the throne, perhaps even because of it, many of the liberal members of the upper class looked on the beginning of his reign as the dawn of a new age. Those of his associates who were not enthusiastic progressives anxious to adapt to Russian use the best ideas of the American and French revolutions were at least enlightened conservatives trying to improve the old Russian methods of administration, and so constitutional plans of a wide range of political complexion were before the dazzling prince. Of outstanding symmetry and cleverness were the schemes of M. M. Speransky, who proposed an integrated structure of legislative, executive and judicial government reaching from the highest level to the lowest under the beneficent legal autocrat. In architectural splendour Speransky had perhaps approached the framers of the American constitution, but although for a moment an attempt at the impossible seemed likely, that is, to make a reality of the edifice, Speransky was soon pushed into the background, then into disgrace, as Alexander turned to face the threat of Napoleon, avert it and then defeat it, setting off to seek wider glory on the European stage, leaving behind him a government less than half reformed and only partly improved.

In 1814 Alexander led his troops into Paris, and this experience could hardly fail to develop in him something of a Messianic outlook on the international problems of Europe. Peter the Great's defeat of Sweden at the beginning of the eighteenth century had served notice on the other continental powers that Russia was henceforth to play an important part in their wars and diplomatic exchanges. The Seven Years War had brought Russian troops to Berlin, and taken their threat several steps further. Catherine had swallowed up more than her fair share of Poland, and established Russia on the Black Sea. And now, after the brief uneasy Tilsit peace, the deep anxiety but final triumph of 1812, the Tsar had become one of the arbiters of Europe. Russia's imperial interests were not directed exclusively westwards, as we have already seen, and she continued to struggle with her traditional enemies to the south, the Turks and their allies. By 1815 Russia was established not only on the Black Sea but also in Georgia, and had moved up to the Danube and nearer her age-old objective, Constantinople. She was continuing her penetration across Siberia into Alaska and down to Central Asia too, and settling the area behind her widened boundaries. New provinces were developed to the south, for example, where immigrants from Germany and elsewhere accepted the invitation to come in and make their living on a larger scale than that to which they had been accustomed.

Just before the Vienna settlement brought the Napoleonic era to a close, the Treaty of Ghent of 1814 concluded the war between Great Britain and the United States, after an earlier offer of the Emperor Alexander to mediate between the two had not been taken up. The 1812 war had given the American army and navy great cause for pride in the post-war battle of New Orleans and engagements on the Great Lakes, and came to be known as the second War of Independence. Without denying the glory of either the first or second such war, historical accuracy demands the observation that on each occasion the United States benefited greatly from her exploitation of a crisis in Europe. Loans from France and Holland, the intervention of the French navy, the organisation by Catherine the Great of the Armed Neutrality, all of them motivated by hostile feelings towards Great Britain, helped America along the road to the attainment of the aims declared in 1776. Franklin and his associates cleverly exploited European rivalries to gain favourable terms in the Peace of Paris. And then, in 1812, Great Britain was preoccupied with her struggle against Napoleon and could not worry very much about her transatlantic troubles, which she had largely if necessarily brought upon herself by interfering with the rights of neutral American shipping.

The war of 1812 also reflected the influence of a new aggressive force in American politics, the 'war-hawks' of the west, with a lust for land in Canada, which had been far from sated in the first War of Independence. Held back officially at least, at the mountain Proclamation Line of 1763 until their breakaway from Great Britain, the Americans soon swept into the Middle West. Kentucky and Tennessee entered the Union in 1792 and 1796, Ohio in 1803. This expansion was dwarfed by the purchase from a harassed Napoleon of Louisiana, also in 1803. Lewis and Clark, Pike and other explorers in the American West equalled the feats of Bering, Shelikhov, Baranov and their like in Siberia and Alaska. Americans entered the Oregon country, assimiliated the Michigan Territory, and took Florida from the moribund Spanish Empire. Explaining this last acquisition to Tsar Alexander in St Petersburg, the American Minister, J. Q. Adams, received the accommodating reply 'Everybody is getting a little bigger, nowadays'.

In the case of the United States and Russia the growth was not only territorial but economic and cultural too. Their expanding international influence was a reflection of domestic development in several directions, to which our attention must now be turned. In 1790, a few years after she gained her independence, America had a population of nearly 4 million, only 2 per cent of its present size, but a great advance from the less than a million and a half at which it stood in 1750. In 1795 the Russian population was getting on for 37½ million, about 17 per cent of the Soviet people today, and a considerable jump from the 23 million plus at which it has been calculated for 1762. In the 1790s there were more than 25 million Frenchmen and not many less than 15 million Britons. The nascent American nation, then, was small in population by contemporary western standards, and the Russian Empire large. Both societies were to expand greatly in the nineteenth and twentieth centuries, but the U.S.A. had much further to go and depended much more on immigration, while Russia owed a not insignificant part of her increase to the incorporation of peoples of Slavic, Turkic and other origin.

Americans and Russians, like everybody else in the world in the eighteenth century, were not predominantly city dwellers. In 1790 just over 5 per cent of Americans lived in towns with populations of over 2,500, rather more than 3 per cent in the six towns which had more than 8,000 inhabitants: Philadelphia, New York, Boston, Charleston, Baltimore and Salem. All six of these towns, it will be noted, were eastern ports. Russia's urban dwellers at about the same time have been calculated as a percentage of the total varying from 3·6 to 8·3, the discrepancy in these calculations being the result of difficulties of definition. For example, are 'unofficial townsmen' (i.e. transient or permanently settled peasants) to be included; and what is a town? Moscow contained about 400,000 people, as opposed to the 42,500 of Philadelphia, America's largest city; St Petersburg had about 200,000; and three other towns – Riga, Kronstadt and Astrakhan – had more than 30,000, as opposed to America's one besides Philadelphia – New York. As far as distribution of the population as a whole was concerned, over 90 per cent of the American people were still east of the Alleghenies in 1790, the numerically largest states being Virginia, Pennsylvania, North Carolina, Massachusetts and New York. Just over half of all Americans were in the northern states, just under half in the southern. In the same year most Russians lived in the central industrial and agricultural regions, with the left-bank Ukraine and middle Volga following these as areas of concentration. In their movement Americans mostly started from the eastern seaboard and then moved westwards, while Russians, on the whole, started from the centre and radiated outwards.

Most of the people in both societies were of course farmers, engaged in an extensive kind of agriculture on land which had often been carved out of the forest or taken over from an uncultivated wilderness. As well as small-scale units there were large-scale in America and Russia, with the southern slave plantation bearing certain resemblances to the estate of a prosperous Russian noble. The biggest difference between the two systems, however, was that Americans tended to work free family farms whereas Russian agriculture was based upon communal serfdom. While American settlers were able to establish themselves in new lands on the basis of the Land Ordinance of 1785, which arranged for regular survey and distribution, the Russian Government had no coherent settlement policy and often gave large chunks of land, empty or populated, to powerful individuals who would develop them on their own account. A certain amount of immigration, from Germany and elsewhere, was encouraged towards the end of the eighteenth century, and the Cossacks were a semi-free cutting edge for the frontier, but the serf pattern tended to superimpose itself even on the periphery as it became inhabited.

Serfdom, of course, was not the only reason for the poor productivity of Russian agriculture: soil and climatic conditions were also responsible. American geographical conditions were better, but both American and Russian farming were held back by technological backwardness, and organisations for the proselytisation of modern methods were not reaching a very wide public. This was almost as much the case with the Society for the Promotion of Agriculture, of Charleston, and the Philadelphia Society for Promoting Agriculture, both founded in 1785, as it was for the Free Economic Society for the Encouragement of Agriculture and Good Husbandry, founded in St Petersburg in 1765. Ploughs were still primitive and fertilisers little used, for all the recommendations of the societies in both countries. Technological progress made an impact on the U.S.A. before it influenced imperial Russia, however, the outstanding example being the cotton gin, which led to a steep rise in southern cotton production at the end of the eighteenth century. Wheat was next to cotton as a market crop, and the seaboard middle colonies were its first chief producers. Corn (maize) was grown everywhere, sugar and rice were cultivated in specific areas, the coast of the Carolinas and Georgia. In Russia too there was regional specialisation: hemp and flax in the north-west, grains in the black-earth region, for example. Newer crops, potatoes, tobacco and wheat, had not yet become very popular with Russian farmers.

Because of the climatic and soil conditions and increasing demand, many Russian peasants occupied themselves with manufacturing in the off-season and sometimes full-time, both on a household and factory basis. Textiles predominated in the industrial centre around Moscow, but there was some metal industry there too. The centre of the metal industry was of course the Urals, where more iron was produced than anywhere else until Great Britain overtook Russia at the turn of the century. Many Soviet historians agree that Russia made her entry into the manufacturing stage of capitalism in the 1760s, although it was to be another century before the industrial phase was reached. American industry was able to move forwards after the first War of Independence, and was given a further boost by embargo policies adopted during the second. Manufactures were still the main imports, however, while cotton was soon to be the chief export. Foreign trade was predominantly with Europe, and the United Kingdom remained the chief supplier and customer. Meanwhile, from east to west, from south to north and back again, by sea, river and overland, the busy lines of national commerce were drawn. Russia's internal trade, like America's, was probably more important than foreign trade. Like America's, too, Russia's foreign trade was mostly with Europe and particularly with Great Britain. Towards the end of the eighteenth century nearly half her exports were in metals and textiles, followed by raw materials such as hemp, flax, timber, hides, furs and cordage. Luxury items predominated among the imports. Russia's foreign trade was mostly in the hands of foreigners, hampered by this circumstance and by the poor quality of national communications, much inferior to those available to contemporary Americans, even though Catherine's government devoted over 5 per cent of its expenditure of 79 million roubles in 1795 to this problem.

The Russian government at this time spent 36 per cent of its money on itself, 28 per cent on the army and 9 per cent on the navy, 13.5 per cent on the court and 1.5 per cent on education and welfare. One of Catherine's less beneficial legacies to the Russian Empire was an unbalanced budget, for state income in 1795 amounted to 56 million roubles. Those who talk of Catherine's profligacy, however, should bear in mind that by 1817 the debt had increased to over 1,200 million paper roubles. Nearly half of the state income in 1795 came from direct taxes, mainly the poll tax, and over 30 per cent came from the indirect levy on the sale of alcoholic drinks to commoner consumers. At her death the total public debt was just over 200 million paper roubles. Central banking and finance were probably not as well ordered in Russia at the turn of the century as in the United States, where they had been put on a firm footing by Alexander Hamilton. With his recommendations for the funding of foreign and domestic debts at par, the assumption of the war debts of the states, and the foundation of the Bank of the United States, Hamilton gave the federal government of the U.S.A. the confidence of its creditors at home and throughout the world. Customs duties and an excise tax, the latter by no means popularly received, provided the money to pay off the debts and to keep the government solvent. Like the Russian budget, the American was unbalanced towards the end of the eighteenth century, although not to the same extent. In the 1790s the average income was $5,717,000 and the average expenditure $5,776,000. In the first decade of the nineteenth century, however, the budget was increased but balanced, $13,056,000 coming in and $9,086,000 going out. Like Russia, America was to be closely acquainted by 1815 with the evils of paper money. But post-Keynesian historians must not be pre-Keynesian in their historical judgements, and must recognise the benefits of paper inflation, even of unbalanced budgets.

In the age of the democratic revolution both the American and Russian economies were showing signs of self-reliance and growth. Already both were playing an important part in world commerce, and although there were large patches of static subsistence in them, their internal markets were already linked up and absorbing much of the national energy at home. Government policies in both economies tended to be *laissez-faire*, in the spirit of the age, although historic tradition made the tendency weaker in Russia than in America. This in fact meant advantages for plantation owners, land speculators and the nascent bourgeoisie in the United States, and for the nobility, merchant class and enterprising members of the peasantry in Russia. Mobility was possible in both societies, but was greater in America. The larger part played by the state and the bureaucracy in Russia made it somewhat more difficult for the enterprising merchant or peasant to make his way there, although the lack of primogeniture and entail made it all too easy for a noble family to rise and decline within the space of a very few generations. Ruin and prosperity were freely available to all American citizens, at least in theory. A fruitful comparison, revealing different attitudes to the questions of private enterprise and frontier expansion, could be made between the organisation and purposes of Russia's Russian–American Company and Astor's American Fur Company.

During the age of the democratic revolution Russia and America strove to develop a culture as well as an economy independent of Europe. In 1783, for example, a young schoolmaster, Noah Webster, announced that 'America must be as independent in *literature* as she is in *politics*, as famous for *arts* as for *arms*'. Webster's own major contribution to this desideratum first appeared in the same year and sold about 20 million copies before his death in 1843. This was *A Grammatical Institute of the English Language* (later *American Spelling Book*), the second in a trio of great American schoolbooks, the first being the *New England Primer*, first compiled in 1683 and running into 6–8 million copies in the next century and a half, and the third being the *McGuffey Readers*, of which over 100 million copies were purchased between 1836 and 1900. The success of Webster's book, as well as that of the *New England Primer*, showed that American literacy was quite high at the beginning of the nineteenth century. New England townships nearly all supported elementary schools, and while no other region laid quite such a solid foundation as this, no settled area was without at least some educational facilities, a wise provision of the Land Ordinance of 1785 reserving a section of each township for the maintenance of public schools. At the higher end of the scholastic ladder there were nine colleges in the thirteen colonies in 1775, and the number increased quite rapidly after independence.

Bureaucratic Russia provided the following figures for the educational situation in the Empire in the 1790s:

Institution	Number	Attendance
Universities and gymnasia	3	1,338
Major schools	49	7,001
Minor schools	239	15,209
Private boarding schools	48	1,125
Military academies	5	1,980
Noble boarding schools	8	1,360
Church seminaries and schools	66	20,393
Medical schools	3	270
Soldiers' schools	116	12,000
Mining schools	2	167
Academy of Arts	1	348
Other schools	9	765
Totals	549	61,956

These figures show a great rise from those for the educational situation at the beginning of the eighteenth century, but obviously reveal that very few Russians were at school in the 1790s compared with Americans. Another discrepancy can be seen in the small part allowed to private initiative and the large part played by the central government in the Russian situation, which was the reverse of the American.

A comparable figure to Noah Webster might be N. I. Novikov, an editor of satirical journals modelled on the *Spectator*, and then, under the influence of freemasonry, a philanthropic humanitarian publisher. Making use of a decree of 1783 which permitted private individuals to own printing presses, Novikov took over several printing establishments, adding them to the Moscow University Press, which he had started to manage in 1779. In six years of Novikov's administration this press issued over 400 titles, more than it had previously issued since its foundation. Novikov's books and influence spread to the remotest provinces, although his circulation figures never matched those of Webster and probably rarely exceeded 1,000 for any single title. In 1791 Novikov's publishing operations were stopped and he was then arrested for heresy, fraud and treason. For even though the Empress Catherine had at first allowed more intellectual freedom in Russia than there had ever been before, the weight of authoritarian tradition combined with her personal annoyance and the French Revolution's influence to suppress it completely at the end of the reign.

Even in America, of course, the age of the French Revolution was not one in which the liberties included in the first ten amendments to the constitution were fully respected. Jefferson was under suspicion as the American agent for a world-wide conspiracy to overthrow good order; about twenty-five suspects, most of them editors, were arrested. On the whole, however, American culture was allowed to bloom in a much freer atmosphere than Russian. All the same Russia and America were members of the same cultural world in the age of enlightenment and the democratic revolution. Voltaire did not cut much of a figure in Asia and Africa; he did at the transoceanic and transcontinental frontier of the European metropolis. At their highest level both frontier societies were producing disciples of the new movements who deserve to be placed in the front rank of contemporary intellectuals and who were fully aware of each others' existence.

The outstanding figures were perhaps Benjamin Franklin and Michael Lomonosov, both polymathic in their interests and achievements. Franklin was a scientist, a journalist and a diplomat. Lomonosov was also a scientist, and a poet, historian and philologist as well. Lomonosov, although of peasant origin, became professor of chemistry at the Academy of Sciences in St Petersburg and then helped found Moscow University. Franklin, on the other hand, had little connection with institutional education, having picked up much of his knowledge in the newspaper office and spending little time in colleges even in his maturity, even though he did help found the University of Pennsylvania. Although their backgrounds and careers were different, both appear to have used intuitional approaches to the problem of atmospheric electricity, in which they had a common interest. Lomonosov has been unjustly accused of plagiarising

Franklin; in any case his achievements in other fields are enough by themselves to justify his stature, although they have been neglected by Western historians.

At a somewhat lower level of achievement there were many in America and Russia conversant with the latest intellectual developments and comparable in their outlooks. Andrei Bolotov, a Tula agronomist, rhapsodises about the simple rural life as does Jonathan Boucher, a Virginia clergyman, in a manner which could only be adopted by those who had known the counter-attractions of urban life. The deist, physiocratic, masonic and other groups of ideas were received in both America and Russia. Learned societies and journals flourished on both frontiers. At the same time, of course, earlier traditions were still influential. Orthodoxy, reformed and schismatic, Slavic folk-lore and superstition maintained some sort of hold on even the most enlightened of Russians, and kept the vast majority in their full thrall. The Puritan legacy was a vital one for New England and, to a lesser extent, for the rest of America as well.

Neither American nor Russian culture could be called independent and self-reliant at the dawn of the nineteenth century. Foreign authors, predominantly British in the case of America, mainly French and German in that of Russia, continued to be more popular than the domestic products. Few American or Russian patriots today would read most of their eighteenth-century men of letters with any real pleasure.

However, this was an extremely important period in the formation of the respective national ideologies, particularly the American. The Declaration of Independence and the Constitution were both produced in this period, when few Americans lived in towns, when few had crossed the Alleghenies. Both documents have a vital relevance for the urbanised, continental U.S.A. of today and for the wider world, nevertheless. Take, for example, the second paragraph of the Declaration of Independence, which runs:

We hold these truths to be self-evident, that all men are created equal, that they are endowed by their creator with certain inalienable rights, that among these are life, liberty and the pursuit of happiness. That to secure these rights governments are instituted among men, deriving their just powers from the consent of the governed. That whenever any form of government becomes destructive to these ends, it is the right of the people to alter or abolish it, and to institute new government, laying its foundation on such principles and organizing its powers in such form, as to them shall seem most likely to effect their safety and happiness.

Magnificent, timeless and universal though most of these remarks are, they have been coupled with other Jeffersonian observations such as 'That government is best which governs least' to form a support for privilege and to deny more recently enunciated freedoms, such as that from want. Similarly, although the Constitution remains a great compliment to the good sense and rationality of the eighteenth century, its checks and balances have been exploited to delay necessary reforms as well as used to avert dictatorship. In the presidential election of 1968 there were strong fears that the electoral college would prove to be a dangerously outdated institution. The problem of what is fixed and what is flexible in the ideology and framework of government developed nearly two centuries ago is fundamental in the troubled society of the U.S.A. at the present time.

As for imperial Russia, an attempt was made in the course of the eighteenth century to add a secular rationale to its older religious ideology. Following a tradition encouraged by Peter the Great, Catherine argued that the autocrat was the sole person above factional disputes and that the bureaucracy acted as an intermediary between the government and the people. She thus helped prepare the way for the more elaborate apologies for autocracy that were produced in the early nineteenth century.

3 Two Great Nations, 1815–1850

Alexis de Tocqueville, in his *Democracy in America*, first published in 1835, wrote:

There are, at the present time, two great nations in the world which seem to tend toward the same end, although they started from different points: I allude to the Russians and the Americans. Both of them have grown up unnoticed; and while the attention of mankind was directed elsewhere, they have suddenly assumed a most prominent place among the nations; and the world learned their existence and their greatness at almost the same time.

All other nations seem to have nearly reached their natural limits, and only to be charged with the maintenance of their power; but these are still in the act of growth; all the others are stopped, or continue to advance with extreme difficulty; these are proceeding with ease and with celerity along a path to which the human eye can assign no term. The American struggles against the natural obstacles which oppose him; the adversaries of the Russian are men; the former combats the wilderness and savage life; the latter, civilisation with all its weapons and its arts; the conquests of the one are therefore gained by the ploughshare; those of the other by the sword. The Anglo-American relies upon personal interest to accomplish his ends, and gives free scope to the unguided exertions and common sense of the citizens; the Russian centres all the authority of society in a single arm: the principal instrument of the former is freedom; of the latter servitude. Their starting-point is different, and their courses are not the same; yet each of them seems to be marked out by the will of Heaven to sway the destinies of half the globe.

De Tocqueville could not be completely accurate in his observations or his forecasts. For example, all other nations had by no means finished their growth; indeed, they had barely begun it. His remarks on frontier expansion were not exact. To some extent Grimm, Deane and others had anticipated him. Undoubtedly, however, there was an impressive breadth and depth of vision in de Tocqueville's declaration, whose principal message we must now go on to examine. In what ways had Russia and America 'suddenly assumed a most prominent place among the nations'?

From 1815 onwards both Russia and the U.S.A. enjoyed a decade or so of comparative political stability. An 'era of good feelings' followed the end of the Napoleonic period in the U.S.A.; while geniality was not so widespread in Russia, there was no major disturbance of the internal peace before the death of Alexander I. At the same time, however, ripples of the age of the democratic revolution were felt in both countries. In the Empire, just as the 1917 revolution was preceded by an attempt to adapt Marxist ideas for the purposes of the Tsarist state, so the Decembrist outbreak was anticipated by the adaptation of some of the principles of the American and French revolutions towards the same end, although there was now little of the earlier official enthusiasm in this endeavour. Having started off his reign in a blaze of liberal and high-sounding sentiment, under the influence of Napoleon and Jefferson, Alexander finished it in an inert, reactionary mood, compounded by a transition from an outward-looking desire for the salvation of his country to a mystical, introverted pursuit of the salvation of his soul. The alienation from Tsarism of a section of the nobility which remained more faithful to the revolutionary principles now led to the abortive Decembrist uprising. What was intended to be a spring of freedom turned out after an hour of confusion to be a further, even deeper period of reaction under Nicholas I. The Decembrists failed because they could not agree among themselves about what they were trying to do, and because there was no social basis for their action.

In Russia there had been a half-hearted attempt to introduce democracy from above; at about the same time it was arriving in the United States from below, thrusting to the top for the first time a true man of the people, Andrew Jackson. The west, which had shown itself as a political force in the 'war-hawk' group of 1812, now produced its first president, overwhelming the Virginia dynasty and the Massachusetts alternative. But not only the west supported Jackson; so did the workers and 'expectant capitalists' of the east, as well as the adherents of traditional Jeffersonianism. Before the election of 1828, which the ensuing arrival of tobacco-chawing ultramontanes at the White House tended at the time to make appear more of a revolution than it does in retrospect, the aforementioned 'era of good feelings' produced a certain amount of political retrenchment after the excitement of the revolutionary era. When conservatism could not be found in the executive branch of the government, it was found in the judiciary, where John Marshall was taking a critical attitude towards almost every question except that of his own credentials. States' rights, those of the legislative and executive arms of government, all fell before him as the federal courts carried on an encroachment of considerable proportions on the basis of the rather sketchy powers attributed to them in the constitution, interpreted by Marshall to form something more like a finished portrait.

Andrew Jackson, although born in a log cabin, had known domiciles of greater luxury and seats more comfortable than the saddle on his way to the padded armchairs of the White House. While he had certainly been responsible for the death of both skins and coats of red before becoming president, he had also been involved in the less adventurous but more remunerative malpractice of land speculation, and had attempted to see the law observed as well as succeeding in breaking it. In short he was far from being the simple frontiersman that he and his supporters made him out to be. Nor were the eight years of his presidency quite such a departure from precedent as has sometimes been made out. His attacks on South Carolina and its spokesman, John C. Calhoun, were in the centralising wake of Marshall, the executive now emulating the judiciary in its suppression of states' rights. His war with the United States Bank was not so much against a bad principle as against a collection of bankers with whom he shared a strong mutual antipathy. His hatred for Biddle was similar to earlier dislike of Robert Morris and his gang of Philadelphia financiers during the revolutionary era. It is as important, then, to see Jackson as the heir to an evolving tradition as well as the creator of a new and powerful democratic government. During the administrations of his successors sectionalism was overwhelmed by expansionism, and the bank question was swamped in a similar manner, at least after the panic of 1837. The sectional issue, coupled with the slave issue, returned with greater force towards the end of the 1840s, however, and the south's peculiar institution was attacked and defended as never before in the debate leading up to the great compromise of 1850.

By 1850 abolitionism had gained ground in Russia as well as in the United States. Officially encouraged by Nicholas I, as long, that is, as it was made as secretly as possible, the attack on serfdom took the form of interminable discussions in committees, apart, of course, from sporadic outbreaks of opposition from the serfs themselves. With five of the Decembrists hanged, and many of the others in Siberia, there were few bold spirits left in the ruling class to attack publicly the institution on which their fellows believed their pre-eminence to be based. Any would-be revolutionaries, and some who would not, found themselves under close supervision from the ubiquitous secret police of Nicholas, which, to convince itself that it was gainfully employed, found incipient treason everywhere.

Nicholas was the militarist-bureaucrat *par excellence*. A parado-maniac by upbringing and inclination, his ideal was an empire in which the serried ranks of his people would address themselves in an orderly fashion both to tilling their fields and fighting their enemies, supervised by a multi-tiered hierarchy in the army and the civil service with himself, a benevolent paternalistic despot, at the apex. The administration handed down to him by his brother Alexander could not fulfil these aims, so Nicholas enlarged his personal chancellery to do a more thorough job for him. A nightmare execution of his dream was the enlargement of the system of military colonies, started during Alexander's reign. A ghastly caricature of a phalanstery, the military colony had its cost and profit carefully calculated and its every inhabitant assigned a special task in the local machine, which was joined, as it were, by an invisible cog-wheel to the state machinery as a whole. Of course, Russian reality during the reign of Nicholas was almost the direct opposite of his aspiration: administrative chaos and corruption, not order and probity; popular suffering, not prosperity; official tyranny, not benevolent supervision. Perhaps the only solid contribution made to political progress in the Empire was the collection and codification of the Russian laws, a task not carried out since 1649.

Autocratic Russia and democratic America seemed bound to de Tocqueville to sway the destinies of half the globe, and both nations were already beginning to reveal great strength during the period from the end of the Napoleonic wars to the middle of the nineteenth century. Beneath the vague religiosity of the Holy Alliance, Russia aspired to be the arbiter of a Europe weakened by long war and political upset. Great Britain, the most powerful nation at the time, grew deeply suspicious of Russia's ambition and the threat posed by her to the Near and Middle East and to India. In a debate in the House of Commons in 1836, Lord Dudley Stuart declared that

But one enthusiasm pervaded the entire population – that of advancing the pre-eminence of their country and its superior power over the rest of the world. The very climate encouraged that feeling. The population looked forward to attaining the luxuries and enjoyments denied them in their own country, but which they knew were to be procured elsewhere. The government of Russia encouraged that feeling. All their policy and arrangements were directed with that view. The moment a soldier left the country on foreign service he received four times his ordinary pay. All these circumstances united made the desire of aggression and territorial acquisition natural and necessary to the Russian empire. A reference to history would show that aggrandisement was the entire object, and had been the successful aim of a country, which, not long since, was scarcely recognised as an important Power in Europe.[1]

Many of his fellow-countrymen agreed with Lord Dudley Stuart, and several of them spoke and wrote the same sort of anti-Russian language. Moreover the flame of Russophobia was fanned by several developments before the conflagration of the Crimean War, mostly in the same combustible region of the Near East. Russia, of course, had been vitally interested in the Dardanelles and Constantinople for longer than the Western powers, which could be seen as interlopers into somebody else's preserve. Russia, it also needs to be remembered, was at least as keen as the Western powers on the preservation of Turkey's integrity, and demonstrated such a desire in, for example, the London discussions of 1840. Such considerations as these notwithstanding, widespread warnings of Russia's ambition in speeches, press and pamphlet led to suspicion on the part of prominent politicians and large sections of the public throughout Europe. Russophobia was intensified by Tsarism's desire to suppress popular revolution wherever it manifested itself in the wake of the French Revolution. With regard to Greece there was some vacillation in Russian policy, owing to the conflicting calls of orthodoxy and autocracy, but no such delicacy needed to be shown in the handling of disturbances in Poland and Hungary. When Nicholas I heard the news of the monarchy's overthrow in France in 1848, he reacted quickly. He had no personal affection for Louis-Philippe, but here was a matter of principle. Diplomatic relations with France were broken, and an army of 400,000 prepared for a march to the Rhine. Such a move would have alarmed Western establishments far more than the manifestations of revolt, and Russia contented itself with the acceptance of an Austrian invitation to help suppress the uprising in Hungary.

The 1848 revolution, like that of 1789, produced a response across the Atlantic as well as throughout Europe, even though the United States tended to turn its back on the Old World after 1815 even more than before. Replying to an offer from Alexander I for American participation in the Holy Alliance, Secretary of State J. Q. Adams declared that 'for the repose of Europe as well as of America, the European and American political systems should be kept as separate and distinct from each other as possible'. President Monroe, like many other Americans, did not see the situation in such a clear-cut manner as this, and in an early version of the famous message for which his name is most remembered, he proposed to acknowledge Greek independence. But the advice of Adams prevailed, and the Monroe Doctrine, as we now know it, was enunciated to Congress in 1823. The Doctrine, of course, had two main purposes. Firstly, Europe was not to expand its influence in the New World, where America would seek to maintain the *status quo*. 'The political system of the allied powers is essentially different . . . from that of America . . .', asserted the President. 'We should consider any attempt on their part to extend their system to any portion of this hemisphere as dangerous to our peace and safety.' (Which other nation, incidentally, would be more likely to have similar feelings of apartness at this time than the other future super-power, Tsarist Russia?) Secondly, Monroe announced that 'In the wars of the European powers in matters relating to themselves we have never taken any part, nor does it comport with our policy to do so'.

In 1823 the Monroe Doctrine was little concerned with Russian [2] and British expansion on the west coast, rather more with European intervention in Latin America. The U.S.A. saw itself as the guarantor of independence throughout the hemisphere. Soon, however, it gave warning that its motives were not entirely altruistic. Pulled into Texas by rugged individuals such as Sam Houston, and worried about European interference there, the government took the Lone Star Republic and then fought Mexico for the Rio Grande and a huge expanse of territory over to California. Victory came by 1848, but not without having established the Americans as imperialistic gringos as far as the Mexicans and their brother Latin Americans were concerned. The U.S.A. paid Mexico $15 million, it is true, but took all it wanted in exchange. Less than a month after the treaty arranging this was signed, Louis-Philippe abdicated, and the revolutions of 1848 began. Many Americans looked upon them as yet another sign of European decadence and the surging power of democracy, but talk of intervention came to nothing. However, if the acquisition of California and the discovery of gold there were not enough to make most Americans look west across the continent rather than east across the ocean, the passionate resumption of the slave versus free state debate more than sufficed to make good the deficiency.

Both the great nations became greater between 1815 and 1850 as their frontiers spread wider. Here again is what de Tocqueville wrote on the comparative expansion of the emergent powers:

> The American struggles against the natural obstacles which oppose him; the adversaries of the Russian are men; the former combats the wilderness and savage life; the latter, civilisation with all its weapons and its arts; the conquests of the one are therefore gained by the ploughshare; those of the other by the sword.

Red Indians and Mexicans would have found it difficult to agree with this statement; so would Russians attempting to cross Siberia in winter. Both peoples, in fact, found natural and human obstacles, although nothing could stop the relentless move of American and Russian migrants across great land distances to the Pacific. Settlers in both societies moved outwards for commercial and religious motives, and both governments supported them, although those disaffected from accepted standards, such as sectarians and schismatics, for example Mormons or Old Believers, would often have to look after themselves. There is a similarity, too, between the movement of Russia into the Caucasus and Central Asia and that of America into Texas and Oregon; in both cases less civilised or weaker peoples were swept aside by self-justifying expansionists. On the other hand Russia's takeover of Finland and Bessarabia and the consolidation of her power in Poland were experiences unlike that of America, which managed to settle the potentially comparable boundary problem of Canada without full-scale war or conquest. Another difference in expansion reflected that between the military-bureaucratic centralised nature of Tsarism and the bourgeois-democratic federal nature of American government. Americans made the great trek without official restraint, and without much difficulty in obtaining land. Russians needed permission to move to the frontier, although some went without it, and some went by force. Thus the Americans were far more mobile than the Russians. Nearly all of the former were east of the Alleghenies in 1790, less than half of them in 1850; the vast majority of the latter in 1850 as in 1790 were west of the Urals, less than a million of them moving to Siberia in the first half of the nineteenth century.

Russia lagged behind in the other great social movement of the century, urbanisation, if not in general population increase. Between 1790 and 1850 the American population rose from just under 4 million to more than 23 million, the natural rate of increase varying around 30 per cent and the rate due to immigration rising to nearly 10 per cent in the 1840s. Meanwhile the Russian population climbed from over 37 million in the 1790s to 60 million in 1835 and 74 million by 1859. Natural and immigration rates of growth were somewhat lower in the Russian case, and the urban much lower. While the percentage of town dwellers rose only slightly in the Empire during the first half of the nineteenth century, 12·5 per cent of Americans were in towns of more than 8,000 inhabitants by 1850 as opposed to 3·3 per cent in 1790, and the big cities of the U.S.A. such as New York and Philadelphia had now caught up and overtaken Moscow and St Petersburg.

The lack of social mobility in Russia was the reflection of a static economy. In the late eighteenth century Russia had been one of Europe's leading economic powers; by the middle of the nineteenth she was falling behind. The reasons for this were partly institutional. Terrified by the democratic revolution, the Tsarist government retained serfdom and was averse to its subjects moving around in an uncontrolled manner. For example, Kankrin, the Minister of Finance from 1823 to 1844, viewed the construction of railways as a danger to public morals, since they encouraged 'frequent purposeless travel, thus fostering the restless spirit of our age'. By 1850 Russia had not many more than 500 miles of railroad, while the U.S.A.'s total exceeded 8,500 miles. For all its great area the settled part of the United States had a railway network as adequate as that of most European powers, while Russia's inadequacy can be measured further by the fact that she had only one-fifth of the French railroad mileage and one-sixth of the German. Russia's backwardness in communications can be seen as somewhat less extreme, it is true, if the vital part played by her waterways is recalled. The Volga, Dnieper and Neva were busy with steamships at a time when, even in the United States, the railways were ancillary to waterways.

Although Russia's institutional backwardness slowed her economic development down in the first half of the nineteenth century, this was also the period during which factors beyond man's control made perhaps their greatest contribution to her slow rate of economic growth. Iron was a basic requirement for industrialisation, and the Urals, the world's chief metal region in the late eighteenth century, turned out to be inadequate to produce a sufficient quantity. Some of the reason for this was the persistence of serf labour, but more important was the maldistribution of natural resources. Charcoal was everywhere giving way to coking coal as the chief means of smelting, and the Urals were deficient in this indispensable mineral. The United States, on the other hand, had all the fundamental requirements for industrial revolution conveniently located in the northeast, and moved quickly into this great change. Of course America's freer social system was at least as much an asset as Russia's rigidly stratified society was a handicap.

The relative insignificance of this aspect of the developmental process, however, might be revealed when we turn to consider the agricultural aspect of the economic question, for one of the most dynamic crops in the U.S.A. was cotton, which was mostly the product of a slave economy. Cotton was the principal cash crop, followed by wheat, also grown for the market mostly in the south. Cotton illustrates, moreover, the tremendous impact that mechanisation had on farming during the period under consideration. Soon after 1800 cotton became the nation's leading export, and constituted about half the total exports from 1820 to 1850. Agriculture provided Russia's chief export in these years too, in her case grain. Amounting to nearly a third of the total in the years following Waterloo, the proportion fluctuated but had if anything risen by 1850. The trade was stimulated in 1846 by the repeal of the protective Corn Laws by Great Britain, still Russia's chief trading partner, as she was America's. Its expansion might have been partly the result of technological improvements in farming, although these were nowhere as important in the Empire as in the Federal Union. Metals and manufactures had shrunk to insignificance as items of Russian export by 1850; imports continued to be mainly manufactured goods, including luxury items. In the American case too manufactures predominated in imports, forming about 70 per cent of them in 1850. Russia's tariffs during the period remained fairly high; America's were kept low by the preponderant pressure of the farming community. In both cases, of course, it needs to be remembered that internal commerce was much more important than external, becoming increasingly so from 1815 to 1850. In the American case domestic commerce multiplied more than five times as quickly as foreign; in the Russian, less than 5 per cent of the grain produced left the Empire, although it was the most important item of export.

Government finances in both future super-powers were inefficiently organised. Both governments were beset by the problem of paper inflation, America's the more so because of the existence there of wild-cat banking. Both governments had a national debt to worry about, but Russia's was much larger, having been brought about largely by the French revolutionary and Napoleonic wars, which did for Russia's budget something like what the Civil War was to do for America's. Russia's debt, which, it will be recalled, was about 200 million roubles in the 1790s and over 1,200 million just after Waterloo, grew to over 2,000 million roubles by the 1840s. These figures are not very exact, and are given largely in paper assignats, which were subject to inflation; nevertheless they can be taken as indicative of a general trend.

Generally speaking, the American economy was booming in conditions of considerable freedom during the first half of the nineteenth century, while the Russian was growing more slowly in conditions of comparative restrain. Social developments reflected the economic. The classes were rigidly stratified in Russia; in America not at all. And yet there was some unofficial mobility in the first case, and unofficial class structure in the second. For example, some serfs were richer than some noble landlords; those with dollars were superior to those without. There were certain basic similarities between the two societies too. For example, in 1850 the vast majority of the population in both the U.S.A. and Russia were living in rural family units, thinking of little more than self-support. In the American case, it is true, farms were single-family because labour was too mobile and it was too easy for an energetic worker to acquire land; in the Russian case because serfdom still exerted its stranglehold, and serf law combined with ancient custom to keep the peasant households attached to the commune. There were nevertheless some rich Russian peasants and some prosperous American farmers, even apart from the plantation owners. This latter group approximated, of course, to the Russian landlord class, and were even more committed to their own peculiar brand of slavery. Yet while the movement for abolition languished and then died in the American south, it grew strong in the north. By no means as sectionally neat, an emancipation movement was growing in the Tsarist state of Alexander I and Nicholas I too, and partly reflecting the growth of the money economy and the stratification of the peasantry.

The Tsars wavered before the attack on serfdom, appearing at times to favour the liberal viewpoint, but for the most part the reactionary. Some changes in the system were allowed in Poland and the Baltic provinces, and for a small group in the centre, but the essential structure of serfdom remained. This was clearly revealed by the continued refusal of the government to put any limit on serf labour or money dues, which could be explained by the fact that the Tsarist state was still based on an alliance between the Emperor and the majority of the landed nobility. Nicholas attempted to strengthen this alliance by restricting future entry into the top class; such a policy would rather hasten its downfall. He equally vainly tried to boost the mercantile middle class by creating the rank of honorary citizen. Government action such as this could do little to preserve indefinitely the social *status quo* in the face of slow but remorseless economic change.

Russian society before the emancipation of the serfs could best be characterised, then, as feudal, while contemporary American society might be considered to be poised between the agrarian power of the south and the rising urban strength of the north. All these labels are extremely crude if not modified, of course. In the American case allowance has to be made for the west, and internal divisions in all three principal regions, for the horizontal split between planters, bourgeois and proletarians, and confusing local adaptation of these three broad divisions. For example, it is difficult to equate a southern poor white with an indigent northern immigrant or Negro slave, although all of them fall into the category of proletariat. The same sort of observation would apply to the Russian situation, where it would be difficult to equate a prosperous central Russian peasant with a thriving Cossack or successful Siberian settler, although they can all be deemed members of the rural middle class or yeomanry.

Social strength and weakness were both clearly reflected in the contemporary cultural sphere, which tended to be dominated by a middle-class outlook in America and an aristocratic attitude in Russia. Applying this observation first of all to the respective school systems, America had come by 1850 to accept in the north-east, and to a lesser extent in other sections, the principle of free public education for all white children at primary and secondary level by professionally trained teachers. Even in the more advanced regions, however, the poor were at a distinct disadvantage. Higher education, even secondary education, was often denied them because their parents could not afford to continue to support a potential bread-winner beyond the age at which he could be earning. More prosperous citizens were opposed to paying for the upkeep at school of other people's children. A second detraction from the surface brightness of the educational picture was the prevalence of a narrow obscurantism which enlightened educators such as Horace Mann found extremely difficult to struggle against.

What was intended not to happen in parts of America occurred by design in Russia, where enlightenment was officially discouraged. The Minister of Education, Count Uvarov, reported to the Tsar in 1832 that the only sure way of keeping out pernicious foreign influences was an educational system founded on 'the truly Russian conservative principles of Orthodoxy, autocracy and nationality, our last anchor of salvation and the best guarantees of Russia's strength and greatness'. For the successful application of Uvarov's principles, an educational policy was necessary that preserved the existing social order by discouraging the lower elements from rising above themselves, and by eliminating all liberal, alien and subversive ideas. To achieve the second aim, Uvarov deemed it necessary in 1843 'to collect and consolidate in the hands of the government the control of all intellectual resources, theretofore scattered, of all means of general and private education that had failed to gain recognition and had partly escaped supervision'. While earlier legislation in Alexander's reign had not excluded the lower orders from secondary education, it had tended to do so. Now in 1845, to attain the first of the aims stated above, an attempt was to be made to reduce 'the excessive influx into higher and secondary schools of young men born in the lower strata of society for whom higher education is useless, indeed, an unnecessary luxury which tends to drive them away from their natural surroundings without benefit to themselves or the state'. Such measures as these notwithstanding, the percentage of commoners in Russian schools rose towards the end of the reign of Nicholas I, when there were over 370,000 pupils, mostly boys at elementary level, in the educational institutions of the Empire.

Literate Russians were still a drop in the ocean of more than 70 millions, at a time when illiteracy among white adults in America was considered high at no more than 1 million. America had by far the greater reading public, then, although she had not developed such a high level of secular culture. During the reigns of Alexander I and Nicholas I, for all the strict and clumsy censorship, Pushkin, Lermontov and Gogol produced their indisputably great work, while Emerson, Thoreau and Hawthorne were rather aspiring to greatness. The reasons for the comparative maturity of Russian literary culture during the period are difficult to establish, but it can probably best be seen as the culmination of a process already detectable in the eighteenth century, for the other reasons – the development of an appreciative audience, contact with exciting European movements, the great boost given to national pride by military victory – are at least as applicable to the United States. Exclusive to the American situation was the inferiority feeling still engendered by the existence and continued liveliness of an older national culture using the same language. Thus Fenimore Cooper was irritated to be called the American Walter Scott, and wanted Scott to be known as the British Cooper. Either way, Cooper did not succeed in bringing freshness to American literature with his use of a new indigenous theme, the frontier, nor did Emerson or Thoreau succeed in creating a distinctively American style nearer the seaboard. Ironically, the more introverted worlds of Hawthorne and Poe are better representatives of the American literary imagination in the first half of the nineteenth century than those created by the more expansive outlooks of the other three. While literary men in America did not have the full confidence to use their own exuberant language in an unrestrained manner, folk tales and songs were unselfconsciously showing how it could be done. Similarly the culture of the Russian peasants was more alive than many measured artefacts of the Tsarist court, and the best writers of the time such as Pushkin and Gogol were beginning to give it their serious attention.

By 1850 America and Russia could both claim to have developed, or at least to be in the process of developing, their own modern secular culture. In a wider sense of the word, this included the formulation of a distinctive national ideology. Official Russia expressed its outlook most succinctly in Uvarov's triad, Orthodoxy, autocracy and nationality, conceived perhaps as a counter to the French Revolution's liberty, equality, fraternity. When the 1848 sequel to the 1789 revolution broke out, Nicholas I lamented that rebellion and lawlessness had swamped central Europe and were flooding over towards 'our holy Russia'. He called on his subjects to declare, as their forefathers had done, 'for faith, Tsar and country'. Slavophile separateness was thus put forward by the imperial establishment as a stimulus to national solidarity and greatness. Meanwhile the United States were developing their own concept of a manifest destiny. The ideals of 1776 and of the new nation based upon them were transformed by 1850 into a rationale for unrestrained expansionism. Life, liberty and the pursuit of happiness were to give to Americans the additional rights to the land of peoples less capable of using them for such high purposes, the Mexicans and the Indians particularly. Even Emerson found no difficulty in making such declarations as the following, from a lecture on the young American read in Boston in 1844:

> We cannot look on the freedom of this country, in connection with its youth, without a presentiment that here shall laws and institutions exist on some scale of proportion to the majesty of nature. To men legislating for the area betwixt the two oceans, betwixt the snows and the tropics, somewhat of the grandeur of nature will infuse itself into the code. . . . It seems so easy for America to inspire and express the most expansive and humane spirit; newborn, free, healthful, strong, the land of the labourer, of the democrat, of the philanthropist, of the believer, of the saint, she should speak for the human race.[3]

The two great nations, then, both saw themselves possessing a unique ideology and an exclusive mission. In this they were not dissimilar from the nations of western Europe, old or new, except in the breathtaking scale of their vision.

4 Interlude in the Drama, 1850–1880

During the middle decades of the nineteenth century, both the U.S.A. and the Russian Empire experienced an armed conflict of great importance, the Civil War and the Crimean. Both wars brought forward the demise of slavery in their respective countries, and speeded up development in other directions too. The American Civil War has been called, albeit with some exaggeration, the second American Revolution; the Crimean War led in Russia to a whole series of reforms, of which those connected with emancipation were only the most celebrated. It is true that the Tsar-liberator, Alexander II, like many of his predecessors, started his reign a comparative liberal and finished it a reactionary, assassinated for his pains, or lack of them, in 1881. And by this time the era of Reconstruction had come to an end in the U.S.A., leaving the south almost as much in control of its own affairs as it had been before the war and replacing the slave problem with the Negro problem. On the other hand many important developments that occurred in both societies between 1850 and 1880 were certainly connected with the reforms introduced in those years as well as with that mighty accelerator, war. These developments accumulated to make the period 1850–80 something of a watershed in the history of both super-powers. It can thus be said to mark the half-way point between the bourgeois-democratic and the proletarian revolutions; a transition from the nationalist to the imperialist stage of expansion; and the end of the undisputed predominance of the agrarian order and the clear announcement of the impending seizure of power by the industrial, less so in the backward Tsarist empire, much more so in the rapidly advancing United States. For this reason I have called this chapter 'Interlude in the Drama'. Let us take a closer look at how this momentous interlude played itself out.

In 1850 a great compromise brought a brief and unstable lull to the troubles produced in the United States by the clash between slave and free states over expansionism. The oratory of elder statesmen, the desire for appeasement and unpopularity of extremism combined to ensure that the nation would survive the only way it now seemed to Americans that it could, half free and half slave. Such an arrangement would have been difficult enough to maintain in a static society, but with the fifties hardly less busy than the forties, it was to become impossible.

Nothing much need be said here about the American Civil War. Suffice it to be repeated only that the long and bloody war between the states hurried on the emancipation of the slaves and the industrialisation of the economy as well as preserving the Union. A passing word should perhaps be said for Lincoln, too, patronising though this is to such a great man. Above all, honest Abe appears to have been capable of combining a patriotic vision with something a little wider in the sense of a general humanitarianism and something narrower, a superlative political talent. Sometimes rather dubious means justified the glorious end; having split rails, he did not stoop to split hairs or chop logic over legal or moral niceties. He was undoubtedly a personality, too, which is more than can be said for most rulers of nations, including Alexander II.

In the Russian case, of course, a weaker personality than Nicholas I was welcome as his successor. To bring the nation out of the Crimean War and to adjust it to the modernisation that the war had made appear inevitable, somebody more flexible than the stern militarist was necessary. Alexander II certainly fitted this bill; indeed, he was prepared to go more than half-way to meet liberal opinion which was pressing for an end to serfdom at the beginning of his reign. If the emancipation edicts turned out in the end to be less complete than liberals had hoped, this was the fault not only of Alexander but also of conservative landlords ensconced in the preparatory committees. The emancipation, like the other reforms of Alexander, was a compromise between those who wanted to introduce a new order and those who wanted to retain the old, thus reflecting the transitional nature of the reign. If the peasants were still to be tied to the commune, burdened with redemption payments and often given an insufficiency of land, they were now free to bring actions in court, acquire property and carry on trades. If the autocracy was not to give up one ounce of its prerogative, the *zemstvo* was introduced in 1864 to give a greater measure of initiative to provincial nobles, and to a lesser extent members of other classes. If Lenin was essentially correct to note that 'the *zemstvos* were doomed from the very beginning to play the part of the fifth wheel on the coach of state administration', they were able to exert an influence on education, social welfare and economic improvement in rural Russia, and to give a boost to the so-called 'third element', medical and teaching staff, agronomists and other technical experts. These were often radical, or at least liberal, in their outlook, and played a part in the stimulation of political awareness outside the capitals. Along with the qualified legal emancipation of the peasants and the introduction of the *zemstvo* necessarily went a judicial reform promulgated in 1864 and guaranteeing to everybody most of the accepted principles of Western law: trial by jury, equality before the law, and so on. Obviously, arbitrariness and corruption were not removed by such enactments, but they do appear to have been reduced. Finally, in the series of reforms of the 1860s and 1870s, as a result of the emancipation and the military disasters of the Crimean War, the army was given a new recruitment and training basis. Tsar-reformer to some extent at the beginning of his reign, Alexander II was certainly reactionary by the end of it, even though he had given his approval to a plan for mild constitutional reform just before his assassination.

In America too reaction set in during the aftermath of its war following an early promise of liberalism. Civil rights amendments to the constitution and political progress for the southern Negro led to bitter strife and some corruption in the period known as Black Reconstruction. Like the Russian peasant, the American ex-slave found himself with legal freedom but an insufficiency of land. Yet it is surely wrong to consider the period from 1865 to 1880 as that of southern reconstruction alone, thematically to cut developments in the south off from those in the north. Since the war had been fought on the principle that the Union was indivisible, historians are obliged by force of arms to look at the U.S.A. during the period as a whole rather than in sections. The 'long hot summers' of the 1960s, moreover, drove home this point even more by demonstrating more clearly than could be revealed at the time that the race problem, the rural problem and the city problem were all closely interlinked, were all reflections of the same attitude towards the role of government in American society. In such a perspective the corruption attending Black Reconstruction in the south, the business and railway scandals, and the chicanery of northern city and state government, the maladministration that reached as far as federal departments, must all be seen as integral parts of the same basic phenomenon. America was taking a big step forwards from a rural, simple society to an urban, complex society, and government at all levels had not yet made much effort to adapt to it. The manner in which this step had been taken, to a large extent through war, also encouraged the breakdown of whatever public morals there had been in 1860.

Both the old and the new order protested about the way in which the transition was being accomplished. In 1867 the Patrons of Husbandry, or Grange, formed together to work for social, political and economic cohesion for those who had previously been isolated. Industrial workers too attempted to organise themselves, most notably in the Noble Order of the Knights of Labor, formed in 1869 and growing to a membership of over 700,000 by 1885. The first great clashes between government and united protest were to come, however, in the 1880s and 1890s.

It was a measure of Russia's backwardness that opposition to the government there in the 1860s and 1870s was to take the form mostly of pre-industrial populism. Not only this, it was a populism not of the people, but for the people by a group of intellectuals. Just after emancipation, peasants reacted violently but rather blindly against the inequities of the Tsar's edicts, many of them believing that the 'true' emancipation was still to come. By no means another Pugachevshchina, the revolts encouraged the populists to think of a repetition of the great peasant war of a century ago, although this time under their more certain control. In other words, in a sense, many populists could agree with Alexander II that 'it is better to begin to abolish bondage from above than to wait for the time when it will begin to abolish itself spontaneously from below'.

Volume I of Marx's *Capital* appeared in foreign translation for the first time in Russian in 1872; Lenin was born in 1870. But these events, of course, could not be seen at the time as pointers to the future. The second event was unremarkable when it occurred; the first occasioned little notice, even from the Tsarist censor. What was a German's analysis of the process of industrialisation to do with Russia? Just as, in an ironical manner, some populists looked upon emancipation as did the Tsar-liberator, so many members of the bureaucratic establishment were looking on Russia's progress towards modernity as did a large section of the political opposition. Both groups saw the commune as a permanent feature of Russian life, both believed the destiny of their country to be unique and cut off from the civilisation of corrupt Europe.

This last belief would have been shared by most Americans too. In their view the New World had thrown off the stale viciousness of the Old. America was manifestly destined to demonstrate to mankind that happiness could best be pursued in a democratic society. Although the persistence of slavery and the manner of its overthrow had given the great dream some hard knocks, the conviction was as yet far from widespread that an ideology formed a century before during the breakaway from imperial control was no longer completely appropriate to a vastly changed American situation.

The war which accelerated Russia's transition was fought against foreigners; that which changed the way of life of Americans was fought between themselves. America fought no major foreign enemy between 1850 and 1880; Russia fought several. However, America was not inactive diplomatically during the period, and even the Civil War has to be seen in international perspective to be fully understood. For the south was relying on King Cotton to command the support of Great Britain and France. The north, although in the person of Lincoln rejecting Seward's suggestion that the states should achieve reunification through war against France and Spain, and possibly against Great Britain and Russia too, nearly did come to blows with Great Britain at least. But sympathy for the southern cause diminished in Europe as the war progressed, and a proposal at the end of 1862 by Napoleon III that France, Great Britain and Russia should join together to propose an armistice and lift the blockade of the south for six months came to nothing. Napoleon, however, persisted with the infringement of the Monroe Doctrine that he had started in Mexico, and Spain attempted to take over Santo Domingo. But Karl Marx and others across the Atlantic as well as those in the north struggled against a posthumous victory for the Holy Alliance. Henry Adams commented on a meeting organised by Marx in London : 'I never quite appreciated the moral influence of American democracy, nor the cause that the privileged classes in Europe have to fear us, until I saw directly how it works.'

Spain was out of Santo Domingo and the U.S.A. nearly in soon after the Civil War came to an end, and Napoleon's Mexican adventure was advisedly brought by him to a conclusion too. Unrest in Latin America persisted, however, and the U.S.A. took a growing interest in the other half of the western hemisphere, particularly as talk grew of an isthmian canal. Another area to which Americans paid increasing attention was the Pacific. In the fifties fast clippers had shortened the distance to the Far East, and Perry had opened up Japan. Long-standing connections with Samoa and Hawaii were formalised by the end of the seventies, after Secretary of State Seward had first drawn up a Pacific policy for the U.S.A., declaring that commerce in that direction had 'already brought the ancient continents near to us and created necessities for new positions – perhaps connections or colonies there'. Few Americans shared his vision and others dishonoured his prophecy by calling an integral part of it, the purchase of Alaska, 'Seward's folly'.

Russia sold Alaska to the U.S.A. in 1867 because she considered that her lines of expansion into North America were over-extended. This by no means signified, however, that her imperialist ambitions were spent. From the Pacific to the Balkans, Tsarist ministers found areas which needed to be taken over. Chancellor Gorchakov declared in 1864: 'The United States in America, France in Africa, Holland in her colonies, England in India, were all forced to take the road of expansion dictated by necessity rather than by ambition, a road on which the chief difficulty is to know where to stop.' In like manner anxiety for the security of trade routes and frontiers, together with Russia's own 'civilising mission', provided a rationale for deeper penetration in Central and East Asia, and continued interest in the Balkans. Moreover the nature of the Tsarist state, a military-feudal bureaucracy, in which generals were very influential and the Emperor saw himself, as above all, the commander-in-chief of his forces, meant that the army was always looking for employment, which would mean fame, fortune and, after 1856, restoration of the confidence that had been struck such a severe blow in the Crimean War.

The Crimean War was a sad chapter for Russia in that long nineteenth-century story which was known as the Eastern Question, although for Russia, of course, it should more accurately be called the Southwestern Question. However it is located, the question became inextricably connected with the movement known as Pan-slavism, which came to something of a head in the 1870s and then burst at the end of that decade. Another war against Turkey, brought to an end in 1878 after a considerable extension of Russian interest in the Balkans, redressed much of the humiliation of 1856, but at the cost of the sacrifice of the ideal of Orthodox and Slavic brotherhood. Pan-slavism, like Pan-Americanism, had from the beginning been at least partly a cover for national expansion, and as such was still to be of some service. At the end of the reign of Alexander, however, the older spirit of the Holy Alliance was in the ascendant with the revival of the Three Emperors' League first formed at the beginning of the 1870s and reflecting both the new strength of Germany and the general imperial desire to protect 'the peace of Europe from any subversive attempts'. Under the latter heading would no doubt have come any recrudescence of Polish nationalism such as had caused a spot of bother at the beginning of the 1860s.

Interlude in their drama though it can be called, the period 1850–1880 was a very busy one as far as the future super-powers were concerned. Not only did they both fight important wars and develop diplomatically, they also extended and consolidated their frontiers, America in the Great Plains and Russia in Asia. Both expanded demographically and economically too. About 23 million in 1850, the American population had more than doubled to just over 50 million in 1880, while during the same period the Russian population rose from about 70 to over 90 million. Almost none of the Russian increase was the result of immigration, nearly half of the American. Immigrants to America, although increasing rapidly in number, still tended to come from old Europe, principally Great Britain and Ireland, and Germany. More than half the American people continued to live west of the Alleghenies, but comparatively few of them, although the percentage was increasing, lived west of the Mississippi, where 70 per cent of the area of the U.S.A. was to be found. The north–south distribution remained fairly constant at a ratio of about 6 : 4, which, since most of the immigrants went to the north, spoke well for the rural south's fecundity. Russian population distribution remained basically static during the period, although the south filled up somewhat. The other indicator of migration, the rate of urbanisation, was lower in Russia than in America. Official statistics show that from the tenth and last revision of 1859 to the first census of 1897, Russia's town population increased from between 4 and 6 million to more than 16 million, that is, from 5.7 per cent to 12.6 per cent of the total. Unofficially, what with peasant immigrants of one sort and another, the town population was likely to be higher, but would still not approach the American figures, which rose from 3½ million in 1850 to more than 14 million in 1880, that is, from 15.3 per cent to 28.2 per cent. In other words, by 1880 more than a quarter of all Americans lived in towns with more than 2,500 inhabitants, as against not much more than a tenth of all members of the Russian

Empire. On the other hand, in straight numbers, there were about as many Russian town dwellers as American.

At the end of what has been called an age of transition, however, most Americans and Russians were still farmers of one sort or another. While the area and total of production increased in both cases, while both societies were affected by emancipation, the basic pattern of agriculture remained the same in many important respects. Florinsky draws the following gloomy picture of Russian peasant agriculture during the reign of Alexander II:

> The introduction of intensive methods of cultivation was effectively precluded by lack of technical knowledge and expert guidance, by insufficiency of capital and credit, and by a communal organisation under which the land assigned to peasant households was subdivided into narrow intermingled strips necessitating a uniform rotation of crops. The three-field system was prevalent not only in the 1860s and 1870s but for decades thereafter; this meant that one-third of plowland was annually left fallow. The use of improved machinery and fertilisers was practically unknown, and the possibility of repartition of land (even though the rule of periodical repartitions was often not enforced) tended to discourage the farmers from taking good care of their fields. The yield of grain was low and remained nearly stationary . . . it failed to keep pace with the rapid growth of the rural population. Idle manpower, however, was firmly bound to the hungry village. The statutes of 1861 made no provision for internal migration. The resettlement of state peasants in the eastern provinces of European Russia, in the Caucasus, and in Siberia . . . was conducted on a modest scale (the number of such settlers from 1831 to 1866 was slightly over 300,000 males), and was discontinued in 1866, when the emancipation acts were extended, with some modifications, to the state peasants. No comprehensive data on the number of settlers are available for the 1860s, 1870s and early 1880s, but whatever migration took place was illicit and in contravention of official regulations.[1]

Florinsky's picture is perhaps too dark for the situation at the end of the reign of Alexander II. According to Lenin, who made a careful study of the subject, nearly 60 per cent of European rural Russia was still being farmed by pre-emancipation methods in the late 1880s, but this also means, of course, that over 40 per cent had changed its approach to agriculture during the quarter-century following emancipation. Landlord agriculture, although still comparing badly with other European levels, managed a yield nearly 15 per cent higher than that of the peasants. The nobles' share of land was constantly falling, it is true, and they were saddled by a mortgage debt which had risen by the early 1880s to a pre-emancipation level of 400 million roubles. Nevertheless the area of cultivation was being expanded, particularly in the south, and railways were constructed to southern ports. This led to a considerable rise in the grain trade, managed mostly by middle-class merchants. The average annual export of wheat, rye, barley and oats rose from about 70 million poods (1 pood equals 36 lb.) in 1856–60 to 120 million in 1866–70, and to nearly 260 million in 1876–80; that is, grain exports nearly quadrupled in just over twenty years.

While the commune and the landlord preserved much of their power in Russia, although it was waning, the family farm remained the basic unit of American agriculture in all regions. Yet there too important changes were taking place. In the south slavery was replaced by sharecropping and other restrictive forms of tenant farming, and the old planter aristocracy, never a large class, tended to give way to a storekeeper, creditor class. In such conditions of social dislocation cotton production took nearly ten years to reach pre-war levels, tobacco production more than ten years, rice and sugar even longer. Cotton continued to be America's largest item of agricultural export, followed by wheat and flour, tobacco, meats and fats. With the opening up of the Great Plains, corn, wheat and cattle all developed rapidly as farming specialities, both in small-scale and large-scale enterprises.

The Great Plains were opened up to agriculture so quickly partly because of the generous provisions of the Homestead Act, partly because of the extension there of the railroad. Both of these factors have been cut down to size by recent meticulous examination, but their undeniable importance stands out in bold relief, it can be argued, when a comparative glance is taken at Russia. For example, consider again the picture of official immobilism drawn above by Florinsky, and then think of the Homestead Act, and the wide, albeit often corrupt, use made of it. As far as the railroads were concerned, the U.S.A. was far ahead of the Tsarist empire in their construction. By 1850 there were over 8,500 miles of track in the U.S.A.; by 1855 less than 650 miles in Russia. By 1880 the first figure had grown to nearly 100,000, while the second had not reached 14,000 by 1881. American superiority in railroads was shown not only in mileage. In mid-century the American railroad was ancillary to the waterway system, which continued to take care of the heavy freight. By 1860 the train had begun to overtake the barge, and by 1875 all but put it out of business. In Russia, partly because of a different river and canal system, it is true, the railroad had not presented a serious challenge to the waterways by the end of the century. Communications require heavy investment, and in both great nations the central government put vast sums of money into railroads. Not all of this money, by any means, was put to the best possible use in either case, and the General Company of Russian Railways, founded in 1857, and heavily supported, like its American counterparts, by foreign capital, did its best to emulate the latter in inefficiency and corruption. Communications developed in other directions besides the railroad during the middle years of the nineteenth century, it needs to be noted. Postage stamps were introduced into America in 1847, into Russia a decade later. By 1870 every town of consequence in the U.S.A. was incorporated into a continental telegraph network. Between 1855 and 1880 the length of Russia's telegraph network increased from just over 1,300 to nearly 5,000 miles. The Atlantic shrank with the successful laying of the Atlantic cable by 1866.

The increasing interconnection of the Old and New Worlds was demonstrated not only by the transoceanic cable, but also by the growth of an industrial economy which stretched from the Urals westwards to California. In the second half of the nineteenth century cyclical business fluctuations in Russia closely followed the pattern of those in western Europe and the U.S.A. For example, Russia, like other European states, suffered from the shortage of cotton consequent on the American Civil War, even though Turkestan was beginning to produce this raw material in significant quantities. However, American industry was of course on a larger scale than Russian during the period. In 1869 over 2 million workers were engaged in American industry, while just under 800,000 on average were employed in fifty provinces of European Russia from 1861 to 1870. In 1879 the American figure was over 2·7 million; from 1871 to 1880 in European Russia, the average was something under 1 million. Moscow, followed by St Petersburg, remained the centre of Russian industry, and the Middle Atlantic, followed by New England, America's centre. Industry, like agriculture, then, was retaining pronounced traditional elements in an era of great change.

In an age of transition and a shrinking world, both future super-powers were still primarily occupied with self-development in the commercial sense, and domestic trade was far more important than foreign. The high tariff rates, introduced by the industrialising north after the secession of the agrarian south, were retained by the U.S.A. after the Civil War, and a movement for protection grew in the 1870s. Yet both powers were still interested in foreign credit, and for this exports were necessary. As Florinsky says, 'Russia's inter-national credit position and her ability to meet her large commitments abroad came to depend on the sale of her grain, irrespective of the price level and of the state of domestic supplies'.[2] The Crimean War had been partly caused by Russia's need of a free trade outlet through the Dardanelles, particularly for her southern grains; from 1871 until the end of the century about half of Russia's exports were represented by grain. Machines, metal goods and cotton yarn were significant imports. Europe was still the principal trading partner for both Russia and America, although Great Britain was losing her predom-inance in the east European trade to Germany. America's exports were still mainly raw materials too, particularly cotton and food-stuffs, and her imports still manufactured goods.

The national debt, war and railway construction, in that order, were the three great items of financial interest in Russia; the railway and the national debt interested the United States much more than war, except during the years 1861–5. The Russian budget was mod-ernised in 1862, excise was substituted for the farming-out of the tax on spirits in 1863, and the salt tax was abolished in 1880. And yet the backwardness of the economy was still strongly reflected in the nat-ional financial structure. In 1880 nearly 70 per cent of revenue came from indirect taxation, and half of this came from the excise on spirits. The poll tax, although soon to be abolished, still accounted for nearly half the direct taxation. Private banking developed during the reign of Alexander II, including loan and savings banking. Private banks helped develop industry; towards the end of the reign there were more than 550 joint-stock companies in Russia with a capital of 750 million roubles, mainly of domestic origin, the great flood of foreign investment not beginning until the 1890s. Govern-ment financiers were very keen to keep the paper rouble stable, but the exigencies of war, involving a tripling of the national debt be-tween the late 1850s and early 1880s, made this impossible. The general tenor of American financial policies during the important

Civil War period promoted the interests of private northeastern capital, which were reflected in the National Banking Acts of 1863 and 1864 and the struggle against greenback inflation culminating in the eventual establishment of the gold standard. The impact of the Civil War is also revealed in the growth of the public debt from little more than a mere $60 million in 1860 to nearly $2,500 million by 1870, a rise of government income from an average of just over $60 million in the 1850s to nearly $450 million in the years 1866–70, and of government expenditure from just over $60 million in the 1850s to over $375 million in the years 1866–70. In the 1870s, it is true, the public debt, government income and expenditure all shrank somewhat, but a great divide had nevertheless been permanently crossed.

Socially as well as economically, the interlude in the great drama was an important watershed in the historical development of the super two. American society in 1880 was still largely rural, but the new urban middle and working classes were the most dynamic. In Russia the nobility was on the decline, and the peasantry was breaking up into three basic strata, but both these processes were gradual. The new classes of bourgeoisie and proletariat were forming in Russia too, but more slowly than in America. The comparative social modernity of the two nations, as has been pointed out earlier in the chapter, can be seen in the nature of their social protest movements at the time; it can also be seen, as will be shown in the last part of the chapter, in certain aspects of the contemporary cultural situation.

By the end of the reign of Alexander II Russia had eight universities with an attendance of something over 10,000 students, nearly half of them working for degrees in medicine; nearly 300 secondary schools for boys attended by rather more than 80,000 pupils, and well over 300 such schools for girls with an attendance of nearly 70,000; and primary schools, which were mainly rural, totalling something over 23,000, with about 1,250,000 pupils, of whom more than a million were boys. For the Empire as a whole, the Ministry of Education calculated that there was about one primary school for 4,000 inhabitants, the ratio varying from 1:3,100 in Moscow to 1:70,600 in Turkestan. Illiteracy was probably over 80 per cent in Russia in 1880, not a lot more than 10 per cent in America. With a population not much larger than half that of Russia, America had a public school attendance figure approaching 7 million in 1870, with primary education nearly universal, at least in some areas, and secondary education very much on the rise. Like that at lower levels, higher education in

America took a great leap forward after the Civil War, because of a greater demand for specialists, wider availability of funds and the introduction of such legislation as the Morrill Land Grant Act of 1862. Following in the tradition of the Land Ordinance of 1785, the Morrill Act set aside a large amount of land for the endowment and support in each state of a college of agriculture and mechanical arts. The number of colleges of one sort and another, not all of them reputable, it is true, ran into thousands by 1880, and the number of students attending them into hundreds of thousands. Even in America, however, progress was regional and not achieved without a struggle. As Lawrence A. Cremin has written:

> The fight for free schools was a bitter one, and for twenty-five years the outcome was uncertain. Local elections were fought, won, and lost on the school issue. The tide of educational reform flowed in one state, only to ebb in another. Legislation passed one year was sometimes repealed the next. State laws requiring public schools were ignored by the local communities that were supposed to build them. Time and again the partisans of popular education encountered the bitter disappointments that accompany any effort at fundamental social reform.
>
> Yet by 1860 a design had begun to appear, and it bore upon it the marks of Mann's ideal. A majority of the states had established public schools systems, and a good half of the nation's children were already getting some formal education. Elementary schools were becoming widely available; in some states, like Massachusetts, New York, and Pennsylvania, the notion of free public education was slowly expanding to include secondary schools; and in a few, like Michigan and Wisconsin, the public school system was already capped by a state university.
>
> There were, of course, significant variations from state to state and from region to region. New England, long a pioneer in public education, also had an established tradition of private education, and private schools continued to flourish there. The Midwest, on the other hand, sent a far greater proportion of its school children to public institutions. The southern states, with the exception of North Carolina, tended to lag behind, and did not generally establish popular schooling until after the Civil War.[3]

As hinted in the above passage from Cremin's book, America's superiority to Russia in education was not only numerical. The philosophy guiding it was much more democratic. John D. Pierce of Michigan declared:

The common schools are truly republican. In the public schools all classes are blended together, the rich mingle with the poor, and both are educated in company. Let free schools be established and maintained in perpetuity, and there can be no such thing as a permanent aristocracy in our land: for the monopoly of wealth is powerless, when mind is allowed freely to come into contact with mind.

Pierce talked of an ideal that would be difficult to attain, no doubt, but his was not exactly a voice crying in the wilderness. On the other hand, in Russia there was wide support in the ruling class for the idea that young people should receive a separate schooling appropriate to their social position. Elementary schooling and no more was enough for the 'lower trading classes'. Secondary education, albeit primarily of a technical type, would be enough for the 'better-off trading classes', and higher education should be reserved for 'the upper class which decides the fate of the nation and charts its future'. Not only this, even the non-technical gymnasia were restricted in their syllabus, a law of 1871 introducing what became known as the 'Greco-Roman bondage', with a heavy emphasis on the classical languages. An official explanation pointed out that too much time had previously been devoted to such subjects as Russian and literature, thus encouraging teachers 'to indulge in generalisations not only useless but at times distinctly harmful'. On the other hand such theorists as K. D. Ushinsky were beginning to realise at least the idea of an educational system adapted to Russia's real needs.

America's educational arrangement was in most respects superior to the Russian in the period 1850 to 1880, but the Russian system produced some great men in a wide range of fields, and enjoyed some surprising triumphs. For example, at the great Philadelphia Centennial Exposition of 1876 one of the key themes was the relation of education to national progress. This part of the show was stolen by displays of tools from Moscow and St Petersburg, 'for these objects showed the West for the first time', according to Cremin, 'that Russian educators had finally scored a breakthrough on the thorny problem of how to organise meaningful, instructive shop training as an essential adjunct of technical education'. As Cremin describes it:

It is said that President John P. Runkle of the Massachusetts Institute of Technology was strolling through Machinery Hall one day when he happened upon the Russian display cases. American education was never the same thereafter. Runkle had been wrestling with the shop problem at M.I.T., and for him the Russian solution held 'the philosophical key to all industrial education'. . . .[4]

Interesting and surprising though it is to find out that the launching of the sputnik was not the first time when Americans were to be impressed by Russia's technical know-how, it would be more historically accurate to observe that American schools attracted more attention than Russian from progressively-minded people in the Western world at this time. For example, the Polish revolutionary Count de Gurowski declared in 1857:

> On the common schools, more than any other basis, depends and is fixed the future, the weal and woe of American society, and they are the noblest and most luminous manifestations of the spirit, the will, and the temper of the genuine American communities and people. . . . Europe has polished classes; learned societies; but with less preponderating individual training, America, the Free States – stimulated, led on by New England, by Massachusetts – they alone possess intelligent, educated masses.

What use were the American masses making of their educated intelligence? How did their literary taste differ from that of aristocratic Russia? Can similarities as well as differences be detected between the work produced in the period under discussion by American and Russian writers, particularly novelists? After noting that I shall be answering these questions no more than partly by considering what have been widely accepted since as the best books rather than those most popular at the time, I shall now go on to make a brief comparison between the work of Russia's great triumvirate, Turgenev, Tolstoy and Dostoevsky, and an outstanding American trio, Mark Twain, Herman Melville and Henry James.

For the reconciliation of the modern novel 'with the essential world view of the epic and of tragedy', George Steiner encourages us to look, not at western Europe, but at America and Russia, and reminds us of D. H. Lawrence's declaration that 'Two bodies of modern literature seem to me to have come to a real verge: the Russian and the American'. Steiner himself writes:

> The history of European fiction in the nineteenth century brings to mind the image of a nebula with wide-flung arms. At their extremities the American and Russian novel radiate a whiter brilliance. As we move outward from the centre – and we may think of Henry James, Turgenev, and Conrad as intermediary clusters –

the stuff of realism grows more tenuous. The masters of the American and Russian manner appear to gather something of their fierce intensity from the outer darkness, from the decayed matter of folk-lore, melodrama, and religious life.[5]

Yet both American and Russian novelists fed on Europe. Some completely accepted it, such as Turgenev and Henry James; some, like Melville and Tolstoy, looked upon it in a completely negative manner. Rejecting or taking to Europe, writers from east and west tended to look upon a visit to it as part of their education, as an indispensable aid to seeing their own society in perspective. For example, Gogol discovered his Russia in Rome, Henry James his America in London. This was partly because both great nations were entering modern maturity and looking for their own image; in both cases the novel participated in the quest. The three Russian novelists were fortunate in that Pushkin and Gogol had prepared the way for them, while the Americans' predecessors were still uncertainly searching for a style. However, continues Steiner, both Russia and America

> lacked even that sense of geographical stability and cohesion which the European novel took for granted. Both nations combined immensity with the awareness of a romantic and vanishing frontier. What the Far West and the Red Man were to American mythology, the Caucasus and its warring tribes, or the unspoiled communities of Cossacks and Old Believers on the Don and the Volga were to Pushkin, Lermontov, and Tolstoy. Archetypal in both literatures is the theme of the hero who leaves behind the corrupt world of urban civilisation and enervating passions to affront the dangers and moral purgations of the frontier. . . . The vastness of space brings with it exposures to natural forces at their most grandiose and ferocious . . . all these encounters of man with a physical setting which can destroy him in moments of wanton grandeur lie outside the repertoire of western European realism.[6]

Tolstoy's *How Much Land Does a Man Need?*, Steiner suggests, could have been the nineteenth-century creation of only a Russian or American. Melville's *Moby Dick*, of which a translation has been published recently in the Soviet Union, has seemed a very Russian novel to some of its new readers. In Mark Twain's *Huckleberry Finn*, the Mississippi attains the universal, eternal quality that Russians have always attributed to the Volga. Tolstoy's favourite book, at one period in his life at least, was Thoreau's celebration of the natural life, *Walden*.

Just as the Brontës' Heathcliff and Rochester possess something in their temperament of the wildness of the moors around them, so the American and Russian heroes contain within them the space, the savagery and all the other larger-than-life attributes of their environment. Dimitry Karamazov surely contains some of the Siberian tempestuousness that Dostoevsky experienced in exile, Huckleberry Finn the doggedness and expansiveness of the river which Twain knew so well and from which he extracted his name. To conquer the frontier environment, iron will and a dauntless stubbornness were necessary. These too are reflected in Melville's Ahab and Turgenev's Bazarov, both of whom find their tasks too great to be carried out within the framework of traditional morality. To achieve 'geographical stability and cohesion', not only inimical nature but human enemies too needed to be defeated. The American Civil War deeply affected such an unlikely writer as Henry James; the Crimean War helped produce some of Tolstoy's first tales and no doubt gave something to *War and Peace*.

A final point of departure for discussion could have been Hemingway's celebrated remark that 'All modern American literature comes from one book by Mark Twain called *Huckleberry Finn*', and Dostoevsky's, that all subsequent Russian literature emerged out of Gogol's *The Greatcoat*. The magnitude and influence of both these works are undeniable, but the primary implications to me of the above remarks are that Hemingway's urge away from civilisation and back to nature was most clearly foreshadowed by Mark Twain, and Dostoevsky's St Petersburg twilight world, peopled with monomaniac outsiders, by Gogol. This is not to doubt that *Huckleberry Finn* was the first great American novel, nor that *The Greatcoat* made a considerable contribution to the definition of a Russian literary style.

Better perhaps, however, to finish on the mundane observation that art basically reflects life, and that besides frontier and size, American and Russian society and ideology were the most formative influences on the literature of the two great nations in transition. An analysis of their middle and other classes, of their concepts of world mission, would be of close relevance to a consideration of their novels. The assistance could be mutual, of course, for in the history of the super-powers the epic quality of their life often approaches, some-

times surpasses, that of their art. How could a Melville or a Twain
do justice to Lincoln, a Tolstoy or a Dostoevsky to Lenin?

To return from the literary drama to the historical, the progress
made by the future super-powers in thirty years or so was pointed
out by Marx and Engels in their preface to the Russian edition of
The Communist Manifesto, published in 1882 and containing the
following remarks about the two powers in 1848 and the years following:

> It was the time when Russia constituted the last great reserve of
> all European reaction, when the United States absorbed the sur-
> plus proletarian forces of Europe through immigration. Both coun-
> tries provided Europe with raw materials and were at the same
> time markets for the sale of its industrial products. At that time
> both were, therefore, in one way or another, pillars of the existing
> European order.
>
> How very different today! Precisely European immigration
> fitted North America for a gigantic agricultural production, whose
> competition is shaking the very foundations of European landed
> property – large and small. In addition it enabled the United States
> to exploit its tremendous industrial resources with an energy and
> on a scale that must shortly break the industrial monopoly of
> Western Europe, and especially of England, existing up to now.
> Both circumstances react in revolutionary manner upon America
> itself. Step by step the small and middle landownership of the
> farmers, the basis of the whole political constitution, is succumb-
> ing to the competition of giant farms; simultaneously, a mass prole-
> tariat and a fabulous concentration of capitals are developing for
> the first time in the industrial regions.
>
> And now Russia! During the Revolution of 1848–49 not only
> the European princes, but the European bourgeois as well, found
> their only salvation from the proletariat, just beginning to
> awaken, in Russian intervention. The tsar was proclaimed the
> chief of European reaction. Today he is a prisoner of war of the
> revolution, in Gatchina, and Russia forms the vanguard of revolu-
> tionary action in Europe.
>
> *The Communist Manifesto* had as its object the proclamation of
> the inevitably impending dissolution of modern bourgeois pro-
> perty. But in Russia we find, face to face with the rapidly develop-
> ing capitalist swindle and bourgeois landed property, just
> beginning to develop, more than half the land owned in common
> by the peasants. Now the question is: Can the Russian commune,
> though greatly undermined, yet a form of primeval common

ownership of land, pass directly to the higher form of communist common ownership? Or, on the contrary, must it first pass through the same process of dissolution as constitutes the historical evolution of the West?

The only answer to that possible today is this: If the Russian Revolution becomes the signal for a proletarian revolution in the West, so that both complement each other, the present Russian common ownership of land may serve as the starting-point for a communist development.

Further answers were to be given during the next half-century, although the great question was not completely resolved even then. At the time, certainly, Tsar Alexander III appears to have drawn the correct conclusion about the future of Tsardom from the assassination of his father in 1881, and Americans were right to think that the assassination of President Garfield in the same year had little significance for the continuance of their federal republic.

5 From Nationalism to Imperialism, 1880-1917

Towards the end of the nineteenth century, according to Geoffrey Barraclough in his *An Introduction to Contemporary History*, world history goes through a qualitative change. Evidence that he produces satisfies him 'that the years immediately before and after 1890 were an important turning-point; but we shall do well to beware of precise dates'. Barraclough emphasises that '*Contemporary history begins when the problems which are actual in the world today first take visible shape*; it begins with the changes that enable, or rather compel us to say that we have moved into a new era. . . .'[1] Although Barraclough's assertion is one that could stimulate much discussion, we can for the moment agree here that in the case of the history of the super-powers, the years from about 1880 to 1917 were of tremendous importance. At the beginning of the period the two great nations, like the smaller European powers in between them, entered an important phase in the struggle for empire; at the end of it they both played leading parts in the denouement of the First World War. But before the denouement, the exposition. This involves developments on the domestic as well as on the international scene, which, however, in an age of imperialism, become increasingly inseparable.

In the previous chapter, it will be recalled, Russia's comparative backwardness was discerned in the nature of her populist movement; in this chapter it can be seen in clearer relief when considered along with its American equivalent. Populism in Russia was to the people, in the U.S.A. from the people. Intellectuals predominated in the first movement, and were largely absent from the second, which sprang from the grass roots. Russian populists attempted to avert the consequences of industrialisation before they arrived, American populists to make a protest for a rural America already doomed by the rise of the industrial city. American populism came to an abrupt end as a serious challenge in national politics with the election of 1896, although the campaign of George Wallace in the election of

1968 made some observers uncertain about this. Russian populism, although entering a decline in the 1880s, lived on into the twentieth century in the guise of the Socialist-Revolutionary Party, and after the revolution with the neo-populist contributors to the great debate of the 1920s. It fell with the rise of Stalin.

Official ideology of the period 1881–94 in Russia mirrored that of the populist opposition. Alexander III liked to think of social relationships as simple and uncluttered. His ideal was a nation of happy peasants singing their inimitable folk-songs, while their 'little father' played a trombone *obbligato* in the rural seclusion of his estate at Gatchina. (An American equivalent would be that of the southern patrician sipping mint juleps while the darkies sang their spirituals.) At a higher intellectual level, a similar picture was drawn by Pobedonostev. Not for him, any more than for many of the populists, the empty shams of Western parliamentarianism, the politics of the huckster and the demagogue. The commune provided more liberty, fraternity and equality for the Russian than Western democrats could ever know. Justice was far better attained without the elongated processes of complex court procedure.

In America, as the open frontier came officially to be closed, the beliefs associated with it remained very much alive. Freedom was as desirable and boundless in the urbanised, industrialised community as it had been in the pioneer wilderness. The corporation was no more than the individual writ large; to tax it or restrain it in any other manner was to infringe the fourteenth amendment to the constitution, which had originally been introduced to protect the emancipated Negro, and guarantee him his life, liberty and property. More generally, just as the industrious homesteader had carved prosperity out of the forest, the hillside and the plain, so today's hard-working office boy would be tomorrow's millionaire. Horatio Alger had joined Daniel Boone as a creator of the national mythology.

While the populists were revolting against the failure of the great American farming dream, a new reform movement rose against the nightmare of the city, the anarchy of unrestrained industrialism. The Progressives were essentially middle-class moderates more often moved by altruism than by personal suffering. Rooted in the drive against the city boss and the political machine, a humanitarian aversion to the miseries of the slum and the ghetto, and, no doubt, a politician's realisation of a new road to success, the new reform movement's influence moved into the White House in 1901 after the assassination of McKinley in the turbulent shape of Teddy Roosevelt. His successor, W. H. Taft, was less of an energetic, self-advertising trust-buster, perhaps, but a more successful one, and reformist legislation continued to be introduced during his administration. The presidential torch was taken up again by Woodrow Wilson, but the First World War, as Wilson predicted, was to bring the national reform impulse to an end. For some people, who did not think that the anti-trust and other reformist legislation was followed up by positive enough action, who were involved in bitter disputes including strikes and violence, it had never begun.

Under Nicholas II the autocracy made a half-hearted attempt to adapt itself to the move towards urban industrialised life taking place even in backward Russia. Jolted into action, it is true, by the biggest outbreak of civil violence anywhere in Europe since the beginning of the nineteenth century, the revolution of 1905, the Tsar and his advisers conceded reforms which would have allowed the monarchy to evolve in a constitutional direction if the lines to the left and right of democratic government had not already been drawn up. The government could not co-operate even with the left-of-centre Cadet Party; Nicholas and his entourage looked with suspicion on nearly all members of the Duma and refused to wager even on the strong Stolypin, who was prepared to ignore the Duma in his attempt to save the Empire from destruction. Russia's entry into the world war, according to most observers, made an already difficult position impossible.

Some historians have argued that, had it not been for this unfortunate accident, Russia could have continued on a peaceful path towards democracy and a modern economy. But, of course, 1914 cannot be seen as an accident from the Russian point of view any more than from the British or the French, the Austrian or the German. No less than the other powers, Russia had been pursuing imperialist policies which were leading to a general showdown. Heavily committed from the Balkans to the Far East, impelled by motives ranging from the economic through the strategic to the personal, Nicholas and his advisers were determined to show the flag wherever Russian interests seemed to them to make this necessary. Warned of the possible consequences of war by the disastrous engagement with Japan in 1904, few of them drew back from the brink in 1914.

Although it was remote from the European imbroglio, the U.S.A.

did not escape involvement in the competition for empire. America must look outward, wrote Mahan, and many politicians, business-men and leaders of the armed forces agreed with him. Their appetite whetted by Hawaii and Samoa, American imperialists grew more hungry with the onset of the Spanish–American War in 1898. Given the opportunity by Bryan to remain true to the founding fathers' disavowal of colonialism, the electors showed in 1900 that they were as keen to take up their part of the white man's burden in Latin America and the Pacific as their contemporaries in Great Britain were reluctant to hand over theirs in South Africa to the Boers. While the Boer War helped to discourage the U.S.A. from further colonial acquisitions, outlets for the dollar were sought to an in-creasing extent throughout the world, and Latin America and the Pacific were ever more clearly seen as important spheres of Ameri-can interest. Still using the New World language of anti-imperialist democracy from 1914 onwards, the U.S.A. under Wilson finally moved to protect America's interests in a manner not wholly dis-similar to that of the belligerents whom he condemned.

Neither the U.S.A. nor Tsarist Russia, however, fits neatly into the pattern of the new imperialism developed by western European nations in the decades leading up to 1914. Owing to the law of the disproportionate development of capitalism, Lenin argued, Russia was the most backward of all the imperialist countries, a land 'in which a modern capitalist imperialism is entwined, so to speak, in a thick network of precapitalist relationships'. Capitalism, indeed the whole economy in Russia, was thus largely, if not completely, sub-jugated to foreign capitalism. Meanwhile the socio-political structure of the state continued to retain elements of medieval despotism, to be dominated by a landowning class, and to depend on the acquies-cence of a huge peasantry and a minute urban proletariat. In Lenin's view, therefore, Russia was ruled not by an up-to-date capitalist imperialism but by a 'military and feudal' imperialism.

A Soviet historian declares:

The West European imperialistic powers, while exploiting Russia as a semicolony for the procurement of cheap raw materials and for the investment of surplus capital, regarded her at the same time as a reserve of military power ready to serve their cause in the event of an imperialistic conflict. In either case tsarist Russia was a valu-able 'ally' of the imperialist powers not as a developed industrial nation but as a 'non-capitalist medium', furnishing not only cheap materials but also the millions of soldiers required in time of war to defend the interests of *Entente* capital. Therefore Western imperialist finance capital, in addition to promoting energetically its own industrial investments in Russia, also extended to the tsarist regime huge loans for the suppression of revolution, for the equipment of her army and for the rehabilitation of her fleet, as in 1906–1909, when France advanced the autocratic regime 4,000,000,000 francs to help suppress the revolution and to heal the wounds of an unsuccessful war. The tsarist regime rested upon the social-economic power of the landowning class, and the latter, in turn, on its vast feudal estates, on the medieval economic and cultural backwardness of the village, and on retaining its supremacy by economic and extra-economic compulsion. The growth and concentration of industry during the imperialist era and the rising revolutionary mood of the working class and peasantry destroyed this social-economic foundation of the power of landlordism and tsarism. In tsarist Russia the contradictions of an advanced imperialism were mingled with vestiges of serfdom and with military and feudal imperialism.[2]

As a client of other European powers, Russia found her development thwarted by them. Foreign investors did not want their monopolies threatened by Russia, Lyashchenko maintains, and therefore discouraged the exploitation of some of her oil, coal and metal resources. Developing their own spheres of interest, the other imperialists denied Russia unrestricted outlets from the Black Sea and the Baltic, and pushed her back from consolidation of her foothold on the Pacific. Turned inwards, however, Russia was able to exploit her colonial peoples in Central Asia and elsewhere in relative immunity. There was no scramble for Turkestan as there was for Africa, and the clash with Great Britain over possible threats to India and Persia was all noise but little action.

Soviet historians have argued that the colonial peoples of the Tsarist regime suffered a 'lesser evil' in their subjection to Russia because they were thus able to launch themselves on the road to prosperity and to establish fraternal relations with the peasants and proletarians of the centre. If this be so, the further argument could be put forward that the dependent nature of Russian imperialism was a kind of 'lesser evil' too, since, as the weakest link in the imperialist chain, it was most likely to snap once the pressures of world war were applied, and the world revolution would therefore commence with the downfall of the Tsarist regime and its vestiges, thus allowing the brotherly feelings of the Soviet peoples to develop in unfettered concord. That entry into war would mean the downfall of Tsarism was no secret to contemporaries. Tsarist ministers predicted it, so did Rasputin. Nicholas appears to have understood his predicament too. His correspondence with Willy and Teddy indicates this clearly enough, so does his suggestion of the Hague Conferences. However, with discordant echoes of the Holy Alliance, the *Dreikaiserbund*, Pan-Slavism, and some anticipation of the League of Nations, Tsarist attempts to establish a world peace were to be subverted by their antithesis, the world war, then revolution. With his order for general mobilisation, Nicholas decreed his own overthrow. And the logic of imperialist development offered no alternative – either Tsarist Russia had to submit to the expansionist ambitions of the Central Powers, or resist them, and the first choice was no choice at all.

While Russia had little room for manœuvre in 1914, America had rather more, but this had been whittled down by 1917, and her entry into the war certainly reflected more than the Messianic pretensions of Woodrow Wilson. In a manner somewhat different from the European powers though it may have been, the U.S.A. was equally trapped in the vortex of imperialism. In 1880 such a forecast would have met with complete ridicule. America had no vigorous foreign policy, and almost no army or navy. Then Congress authorised the construction of two warships in 1882, as concern for American interests in the Pacific and Latin America grew, and further expansion developed from this basis. A little earlier James G. Blaine had formulated an ideological basis for such expansion, a customs union exalted by the label of Pan-Americanism. The other nations of the western hemisphere rejected this offer of their big brother, but the idea persisted; American investors were looking outwards, and were too powerful to be denied.

At the same time, it needs to be noted, the U.S.A. was much more than Tsarist Russia the recipient of European investment; up to 1914 more than $6,000 million worth, mostly British, went to the first destination, while little more than $4,000 million worth, mostly French, went to the second. The degree of dependence, however, appears to have been very much in inverse proportion to the amount received, thus reflecting both the policies of the creditors and the position of the debtors. Certainly by the turn of the century, far from being a client of Great Britain, the United States was beginning to exercise a strong and independent influence on international affairs. After the Spanish–American War had been fought in 1898, American investments were increasingly made from China to Europe. There was no end to American expansionism; Teddy Roosevelt was as vigorous waving his big stick from the White House as he had been leading his rough-riders up San Juan Hill and down again. He took Panama, intervened in Cuba and Santo Domingo, helped arrange peace between France and Germany over Morocco and between Japan and Russia over Manchuria, and sent the American navy round the world to show that the U.S.A. meant business. Some change from 1880.

As in other parts of the world, there were lulls before the storm, but the fundamental direction had been taken. The Atlantic had shrunk, America was closely involved in Europe and other parts of the world as well, economically, strategically, ideologically. While the war did not seem to be America's in 1914, by 1917 large loans seemed in danger of non-repayment. By 1917, too, Germany's submarine warfare had revealed how fragile had become the British naval strength that had helped put teeth into the Monroe Doctrine for so long, and how ineffectual a barrier the ocean had become between the Old and the New World. For historical reasons, as a result of astute propaganda, and because democracy was more to be found in France and Great Britain than in the Central Powers, the majority of positive American opinion was probably with the Allies from the first. And after the abdication of Nicholas II in March 1917, Wilson was able to include Russia in his picture of a war 'for a universal dominion of right by such a concert of free peoples as shall bring peace and safety to all nations and make the world itself at last free'.

Wilson's message breathed some new life into war-weary Europe, and the convoys brought food and troops to render more material succour, at least to the western front. Little relief penetrated to the troops in the east, however, nor were they heartened very much by the overthrow of their commander-in-chief, Tsar Nicholas. Immediately after the first revolution of 1917, the second was well on its way, as certain to come now with the continuance of the war as the fall of the monarchy had been assured by its outbreak. October will take its place in the next chapter, but February must now be discussed as part of the age of imperialism. Quite often historians have argued that February was fortuitous, if not quite so often as they have put forward the proposition that Russia's entry into the First World War was accidental. But 1917 was no more spontaneous than 1914. Sometimes Rasputin's association with the Empress has been blamed for it, but John Brown's with Queen Victoria could almost as well be suggested as a potential cause of revolution. The decision of Nicholas in 1915 to lead the army has been deemed the fatal step, but he could hardly have made worse military decisions than some of the lower-born generals involved in the war or conducted his government better back in Petrograd, nor could he have stood up to the Empress face to face any more than he did by letter. The conditions experienced by the Russian troops have been cited as the fomenter of desertion and disaffection, but the French and British troops in the western trenches would not have claimed to be in a much better hole. Petrograd was not the only city where civilians starved, the Russian *muzhik* was not the only European peasant to grow restless, the Baltic fleet not the only spawner of mutiny. Differences of degree and intensity could no doubt be found in all these phenomena from one part of Europe to another, and probably they were most profound in eastern Europe. There, after all, throughout history, the scale of violence and suffering had been greater than in the rest of the continent. Not only this, a rigid mechanism is a crude key to historical explanation at all times and in all places. On the other hand a flaccid accidentalism is even cruder, and explains nothing. The miseries experienced by the Russian people during the war, moreover, produced revolution only when added to the social instability already present before war broke out.

There has been much debate about the existence of a revolutionary situation in Russia on the eve of the First World War. Strike statistics certainly reveal a situation of some seriousness, although no more serious than that in Great Britain if not seen in context. Whereas in 1907 there were 3,600 strikes involving 740,000 workers, the figures fell to 900 and 176,000 in 1908, and 200 and 47,000 in 1910. But in 1912 there were 2,000 strikes and 725,000 participants, and from January to July 1914, 4,000 strikes with 1,449,000 workers taking part. After the outbreak of war there were only 68 strikes with less than 35,000 workers joining them, from August to December 1914. This sudden decline has been used for the argument that the war gave Tsarism a brief reprieve rather than drove the last nail into its coffin. Even if this be so, there can be little doubt that the war added to social dislocation in the comparatively short run, if not immediately. Workers were brought into Petrograd, which already, together with other large towns, such as Moscow, Riga, Kiev and Odessa, accounted for more than a half of Russia's urban population. And many of the new workers found themselves in such large industrial units as the Putilov works.

The total population of large Russian towns had always been high compared with that for all small-town inhabitants added together. Industrial units had been big since the seventeenth and eighteenth centuries. But this disproportion was thrown into even clearer relief by the stage of industrialisation that Russia was going through at the time of the outbreak of war. This rendered her situation so dangerous as to be critical from the start. Two further points must be added. Firstly, a further detraction from the idea of spontaneity as far as the February Revolution was concerned was the undoubted influence exerted over the workers of socialist ideas relayed to them by Bolshevik and other radical party workers. Secondly, just as the Russain Revolution can be said to have been the result of the chain of world imperialism snapping at its weakest link, so its own imperial chain gave way at its weakest point too. In 1916 in Central Asia, a revolt of no small dimensions broke out against Tsarist recruitment. Just as the Russian troops were to object to fighting for the Allies, so the Central Asians now expressed their reluctance to go to war on behalf of Great Russians. Their revolt of 1916 added one of the last straws to the already failing camel's back.

All the participants in the First World War suffered social upsets, if none quite so great as Russia's. Even the U.S.A., the final major entrant into the hostilities and very little hurt by them, did not emerge unscathed. As Wilson's words just before his war message have been reported:

> when a war got going it was just war and there weren't two kinds of it. It required illiberalism at home to reinforce the men at the front. We couldn't fight Germany and maintain the ideals of Government that all thinking men shared. . . . 'Once lead this people into war,' he said, 'and they'll forget there ever was such a thing as tolerance. To fight you must be brutal and ruthless, and the spirit of ruthless brutality will enter into every fiber of our national life, infecting Congress, the courts, the policeman on the beat, the man in the street.'

Wilson's government made his words come true, introducing

espionage and sedition acts as ruthless as any in the world. Under them some 1,500 people were arrested for disloyalty, including socialist leaders such as Eugene V. Debs. Not only this, an unofficial campaign against suspected or potential traitors meant humiliation and even ruin for German-Americans and others. To make the world safe for democracy, democratic ideals had to be forgotten. Intolerance and persecution were worse after the armistice than before, although neither period produced anything approaching the suffering inflicted on the Russian people by revolution and civil war in 1917 and afterwards.

Imperialism is, albeit to a debatable extent, an economic phenomenon as much as anything else; certainly, to see the period under discussion in the round, we have to have a look at the contemporaneous agricultural, industrial and financial strengths of the future super two. We also have to consider their demographic positions, the number and distribution of their peoples. Russia was subjected to its first complete census in 1897, and this revealed a total population of something under 130 millions. The urban population was now over 16 million getting on for 13 per cent of the total; there were forty-four cities with more than 50,000 inhabitants and five with more than 200,000. Regionally, the Empire's millions were to a large extent Great Russians – forty-four per cent; next, inhabitants of the Ukraine, Poland, White Russia and the Baltic provinces – thirty-eight per cent; finally, mostly Turkic peoples living in the Caucasus, Central Asia and Siberia, and the peoples of Transcaucasia – much of the rest. One notable feature of the distribution of the population in the last years of Tsarism was the growth of Siberia's from 5·76 million, including 4·65 million Russians, in 1897 to 9·37 million, including 8 million Russians, in 1911. Nearly all the Siberian population was to the south, near the recently completed Trans-Siberian railway. Another important trend during the reign of Nicholas II was to the city, while the population as a whole grew to 175 million by 1914.

In 1890 the total population of the U.S.A. was 63 million; in 1900, 76 million; and in 1910, 92 million. The rural population declined from just over 49 per cent in 1880 to just under 35 per cent in 1910, while the percentage of the population in towns and cities over 2,500 in size grew from 29 per cent in 1880 to 46 per cent in 1910. By 1910, only 30 per cent of the American people were yet west of the Mississippi; the north–south split was still roughly in the ratio 60:40.

Immigrants accounted for well over half the population increase during the years 1880–1910, and from 1890 onwards more than half of these were 'new', that is from Italy, the Austro-Hungarian and Russian Empires. The percentage of Negroes among the American people dropped from 13·1 per cent in 1880 to 10·7 per cent in 1910.

American farmers, like their Russian counterparts, experienced great hardships in the period 1880 to 1900, largely owing to the dislocation produced by the industrial revolution. The basic problem in the U.S.A. was that as a result of improved methods of production and communications, and the virtual doubling of the area under cultivation, a tendency set in for production to outrun demand. With prices dropping, the farmers attempted to produce even more, and thus made the situation worse. A second problem, not unconnected with the first, was that of indebtedness, often resulting from tenancy or mortgage. From 1900 to 1920, however, American farmers enjoyed comparative prosperity. The growth of cities increased demand at home and the world war increased it abroad. The Progressives and Wilson sought to improve the credit system, which helped the farmers in the short run, and to make some steps towards soil and other forms of conservation, which would be to their long-term advantage.

Rural Russia's problems were deeper and did not lend themselves so easily to a cure. Possibly the soil and the climate would always conspire against the unqualified success of Russian agriculture. Certainly her social backwardness continued to exercise an often depressive restraint. The peasants were still burdened by taxes and hampered by lack of land twenty years after emancipation, and the new government of Alexander III moved to do something about it. Between 1881 and 1887 redemption payments were lowered, facilities for the acquisition of land by peasants improved, and the poll tax abolished. But the financial commitments of the peasants were increased in other directions, and hardly any relaxation introduced into the stranglehold of the commune.

A useful safety-valve to the land shortage of central Russia was internal colonisation, and the movement into Siberia facilitated by the railway did something, although nowhere near enough, to relieve the intense pressure at the beginning of the twentieth century. This was part of the most celebrated attempt at the solution of the rural problem during the reign of Nicholas II, the reform associated with the name of Stolypin. Stolypin's wager on the strong, his belief that, given twenty years of peace, a class of sturdy yeoman farmers would grow to bring prosperity and social stability to rural Russia, was a good enough plan to cause Lenin some serious alarm. But, of course, Stolypin did not get his twenty years of peace, and he was assassinated while still trying to make his plan work. Estimates vary as to the extent to which his proposals for the consolidation of peasant landholdings and break-up of the commune were successful, but it seems that, on the whole, they were implemented most in the periphery of Great Russia where they were least urgent, and not brought into force very much at all at the heart of the Empire and the problem.

All Russia's problems in the last years of Tsardom were linked together. This emerges clearly when industrial development at that time is considered just after the above examination of the agricultural predicament. As Portal points out, 'The industrial advance before the First World War took place within the geographical framework',[3] i.e. on an historical basis. The chief centres of production were in and around Moscow, St Petersburg and its environs, and certain regions in the Ukraine. The rich mineral deposits of Siberia, for example, had still to be exploited to any significant degree. Apart from the Trans-Siberian railway, there were barely any modern communications east of the Urals. This in turn meant that internal markets were concentrated in areas which were overpopulated, and where demand could not therefore be very high. Unless it encouraged more social migration, then, the government could not expect the optimum rate of growth. In the years 1890–1900, and again from 1908 to 1914, however, Tsarist Russia certainly took several steps towards industrialisation. Production figures in textiles and minerals from those years are impressive. Yet there is no point in arguing that this advance rendered the revolution superfluous, for the war soon showed that Russia's industrial progress had been dependent on the commercial links with foreign powers, particularly Germany. In 1913 Germany provided 47 per cent of Russia's imports, and received 32 per cent of her exports. Among the imports were such important items as machines, machine-tools and railway equipment.

Agriculture, industry and trade, then, were all interrelated in Russia on the eve of the First World War, and a further essential element in the economic complex was finance. Although the Empire was less dependent on foreign capital than before, it was still necessary to her in 1914, and to maintain her international credits she had to continue to export her grain. 90 per cent of her grain exports went through the Dardanelles, a route cut by the outbreak of war. Its sources of financial assistance from abroad reduced, the government also took a deliberate step to reduce its income at home. 28 per cent of the total revenues of the Empire in 1914 accrued from a state monopoly of spirits; from August of that year onwards the sale of intoxicating drinks was prohibited. The government thus cut off over a quarter of its income, arguing that such a drastic reform was necessary because 'the welfare of the treasury should not be made dependent on undermining the moral and economic forces of a great number of loyal subjects'. In this manner the paternalistic government helped to bring about its own downfall.

American industrial development during the same period, 1880–1917, may not have been all that far in advance of Russia's measured from some points of view, but it was way ahead from many, and undoubtedly much more dynamic. Between 1880 and 1916 the railroad mileage more than tripled, much of the expansion being in the west. The first transcontinental route completed soon after the Civil War, the U.S.A. had several such routes by the end of the century and a network connecting all areas of the Union to each other. The railroad encouraged settlement and economic growth at least as much as it reflected them; its importance stands out clearly when reference is made back to the situation existing in contemporary Tsarist Russia.

By 1890 the U.S.A. had become the world's leading industrial power; by 1914 its second financial power. These circumstances alone made America a leading imperialist nation. The two principal reasons usually given for this pre-eminence are the nature and distribution of her natural resources, and the size of area and population. In the present context the second argument is tenable only if subject to some modification, Russia being two to three times the size of America and containing a population nearly twice the total of the U.S.A.'s. As far as the first reason is concerned, the nature of the resources would appear not to be all that superior to the other future super-power's. Distribution, then, would appear to be all-important, both for production and consumption. And distribution is as much history as geography, from some important points of view such as that of population at least.

A further reason for America's rapid industrialisation was the flood of immigration that took place during the period 1880 to 1920, the bulk of it 'new'. Most of the southern and eastern Europeans went into industry, unlike the northern Europeans, who, except for the Irish, had more often than not set themselves up as farmers. This new orientation of immigrants does not seem to have been entirely fortuitous. According to a government report of the period:

> Historically, the American origin of the more recent immigration, so far as such a movement can have a specific origin, seems to have been the desire of certain Pennsylvania anthracite mine owners to replace the employees that they found hard to deal with, and especially the Irish, with cheaper and more docile material. Strikes were a frequent cause of friction . . . and it was natural that employers should be on the lookout for new sources of labor supply. In a number of places these raw recruits of industry seem to have been called in as the result of a strike, and there probably were plenty of instances of sending agents abroad to hire men or of otherwise inducing labor to immigrate either under contract or with an equivalent understanding.[4]

Ignorant and poor immigrants took over most of the unskilled jobs, then, and often as part of their employers' plan. Although unemployment does not appear to have been a great problem before the 1930s, the impact of immigration was considerable; it depressed wages and impeded unionisation. It also made a contribution to both the extent and pace of America's industrialisation.

With the great economic changes in America went a profound rearrangement of society. With the rise of the 'rugged individualist' millionaire, then of the corporation, a new class of industrial entrepreneurs was created. Dependent on this class was a middle class composed of managers and professional people, then came the working class, divided into skilled and unskilled. The gulf in the working class revealed itself in the development of unions. The American Federation of Labor had a membership of 2 million by the eve of the First World War and 4 million by 1920, but it catered for skilled workers only, and not for all of them. Unskilled workers often joined the anarcho-syndicalist International Workers of the World, which aimed for 'the Big Industrial Union'. The nearest approach to this in the U.S.A. was not to come before 1936, with the foundation of the Committee for Industrial Organisation.

About a third of the American population was still involved in agriculture at the time of the outbreak of the First World War, over two-thirds of the Russian. Nevertheless an industrial middle class and a proletariat were new phenomena in Russia too during the last days of Tsarism. A few unions were developed, several strikes were held, and in 1905 and 1917, industrial action of the most vigorous type was taken. The new middle class, for its part, sought to exert political influence and to replace the declining but still powerful landed nobility as the chief supporter of the throne. The rivalry of the old and new establishments, and the temporary *modus vivendi* arrived at by them now and again, have been seen by Soviet historians as an important part of the social basis of the inconsistencies in Tsarist policies in the first years of the twentieth century. Partly for this reason, and less because of weaknesses in his personality, Nicholas swayed between constitutional monarchy and autocracy, peace and war. The supreme autocrat was tossed this way and that by the buffets of an ocean of social and other troubles against which he was powerless, and worn down by a million natural shocks to which he had become uncomprehending heir.

With much more understanding of the great problems facing the Tsarist empire, Stolypin hoped to bring it into the twentieth century with a thorough readjustment of rural society. A less celebrated means towards the same end of modernisation without revolution was the introduction of plans for universal primary education. The census of 1897 revealed an illiteracy level of nearly 80 per cent. Of those who could read, more were men than women, 29 per cent compared to 13 per cent, and many more lived in towns than in the country, 45 per cent compared to 17 per cent. By the end of the nineteenth century almost all educated Russians had come to accept that literacy was an acquisition desirable for everybody, and that universal primary education was the quickest and best means to this end. The implementation of such a scheme was a question discussed in pedagogical periodicals, in most of the *zemstvos* and some of the municipalities, and in the meetings of many private societies. In the Duma various bills on compulsory education were debated and some actually passed. The most important of these, enacted in 1908, provided for the gradual introduction of compulsory free education for all children from eight to eleven years. Since the government was reluctant to delegate any of its powers of taxation to *zemstvos* or municipalities, most of the finance for the new system was to be provided by the state. Less than 100,000 schools existed in 1908, when it was calculated that 317,000 of them would be necessary by

1922, when the plan was expected to be in full operation for eligible children who were likely to number just under 16 million. This was revealed as something of an underestimate by 1914, when there were already more than 15 million children of the projected school age. By this year, according to the 1908 plan, there should have been 149,000 schools. In fact, by 1915, there were 122,000 schools catering for just over 8 million young students. Included in this number were some 30,000 church schools, the subject of considerable controversy in the last years of Tsarism. Soon after the world war broke out, then, just over half the eligible children were at primary school, the proportion being higher than this in the towns and lower in the countryside. General literacy had by this time crept up to about 30 per cent, and probably exceeded 50 per cent in towns. To borrow a term from another field, Russian primary education might be said to have passed the take-off point and entered a period of sustained growth in 1915, but there was probably retrogression during the turmoil of war and revolution.

The nature of the revolution itself, of course, was as much influenced by the semi-literacy of the people as it was by the stage reached in economic, social and political development. Imperial ministers hoped to use universal primary education to instil in the young loyalty to Tsarism. Instead, at the half-way stage, revolutionaries were able to make use of the situation to disseminate their own propaganda. For both sides reading and writing were very much means to an end. So had they become in the U.S.A., where an energetic discussion had arisen in the 1890s concerning the purposes and aims that should be adopted by schools. Even earlier theorists, like Horace Mann and John D. Pierce, saw universal education as a basic necessity of a democratic society. By the 1890s the question had become, what sort of universal education, and for what kind of democratic society?

By 1900 over $15\frac{1}{2}$ million children were enrolled in American public schools; by 1920 over $21\frac{1}{2}$ million. Nearly 80 per cent of all children were enrolled in the schools by 1920, and illiteracy was down to 6 per cent by that year. Massachusetts had been the first state to pass a state-wide compulsory attendance law in 1852; Mississippi was the last to do so in 1918. Striking advances were made in secondary education too. Over $200 million were spent on public education as a whole in 1914, and over $1,000 million in 1920. (Compare Tsarist Russia: something more than 270 million roubles

on education in 1916, a rouble being worth about half a dollar at
this time.) And yet the pedagogical picture did not appear all that
bright to many people in the U.S.A. during the last years of the
nineteenth century and the first years of the twentieth.

For example, there was the problem of the 'new' Americans.
According to a massive study made by the United States Immigration Commission in 1909, getting on for 60 per cent of the
children in the schools of nearly forty of the nation's largest cities
were of foreign-born parentage, covering a span of sixty different
ethnic origins. Not only basic English but also rudimentary hygiene
had to be inculcated by teachers who found their curricula
spreading wider and lower than the three Rs. To encourage the
assimilation of the immigrant groups into the cities, to help rural as
well as urban schoolchildren, to remain true to the democratic aims
enunciated by such as Mann and Pierce, theorists were coming
round to believe more and more strongly that the Progressive Era
demanded a progressive system. A belief in the education of the
whole man was encouraged by the philosophical arguments of James
and Dewey. Public secondary education, still for the comparatively
few in Tsarist Russia, was already being looked on in the U.S.A.
as almost as much a universal right as elementary. Over a million
young Americans attended public high schools in 1910, while the
comparable figure was 600,000 in Russia five years later. Secondary
education was by no means seen as a universal right by Tsarist
ministers, who continued, with a few far-sighted exceptions, to be
weighed down by the exclusive traditions of their predecessors. Yet
an element of democracy was creeping even into the gymnasia. For
example, in the Vilna school region the percentage of the children
of nobles and bureaucrats attending gymnasia fell from 67 per cent
in 1894 to 37 per cent in 1910, while attendance by young peasants
rose from 6 per cent to 18 per cent. At the highest level, as well as at
the lowest, Russia lagged behind America in 1914, the number of
students at the former's universities and other advanced institutions
being numbered in tens of thousands, at the latter's in hundreds of
thousands.

The rise of literacy had strong implications for the writer. Having
felt the full force of frontier expansion in the period between 1850
and 1880, moreover, literature in America and Russia came under
the equally powerful influence of the city too during the next thirty
years or so. The themes of industrialisation and its consequences for

the people come over most clearly in the American realist group of novelists associated with the muckrakers of the Progressive era, but they are also leitmotifs in the stories of Russian writers such as Chekhov and Gorky. While Henry James continues to avoid most of the problems of American society in the less unsettled world of Europe, and Tolstoy turns to internal exile from the urban environment in Russia to peasant simplicity, other novelists concern themselves with the central subject of development in the U.S.A. and in the Tsarist empire.

The 1880s in Russia were a literary lull after the tremendous activity of the preceding decades. To some extent this was fortuitous with the death of Turgenev and Dostoevsky, but it also reflected the great change that was coming to the Empire and of which a clear indicator was the virtual demise of populism and the absence of any philosophy to replace it. With the arrival of Marxist socialism by the end of the nineteenth century, a new set of beliefs had been widely accepted and formed a new background against which the writers of prose fiction would apply themselves to the practice of their art.

The transition is revealed even in the work of Chekhov, a militant non-joiner, who declared:

> I fear those who read between the lines trying to find a definite trend of thought, and who insist on considering me either a liberal or a conservative. I am neither liberal nor conservative, nor gradualist, nor ascetic, nor indifferentist. I should like to be an independent artist – and that is all. . . . Any trade mark or label to me means a prejudice. Sacrosanct to me are the human body, health, reason, talent, inspiration, love, and absolute freedom.

On the other hand Chekhov was certainly not indifferent to humanity at large, nor to progress. His medical training broadened his human understanding, no doubt, and also encouraged him to observe in his autobiography that 'knowledge of natural science and scientific methods kept him on his guard against the writers who denied science and those who attained anything by means of their own reasoning'. He criticised Tolstoy for making remarks on medical subjects when 'he never took the trouble to read any of the books written by specialists'. With the same person in mind, he declared that 'in electricity and steam there was more real humanity than in chastity and abstention from meat'. Obviously here is a mind that might well have had sympathy with the somewhat later statement that Communism was electricity plus the Soviets. Primarily, however, Chekhov was a great writer, the master of the short story, and although he does not go out of his way to discuss the central themes of the age in his work, they are certainly strongly incidental to it.

With the arrival on the scene of Maxim Gorky, Russian writers took a further large step from their first status as diverters of aristocratic society to their later position as engineers of the proletarian soul. According to Miliukov:

> Gorky himself did not realise at first that in repudiating the old dying Populism he was following Marxism, the new, increasingly fashionable doctrine. It was his cheerful optimism and firm belief in his heroes, who by their muscular strength towered above the peasants, that linked Gorky to the Marxists. 'It is not true that life is gloomy, that it consists of nothing but plague, groans, sorrows, and tears', said one of his heroes. . . . 'Life is beautiful; life is a sublime, indomitable progress towards universal happiness and joy. . . . I cannot doubt it. . . . I have followed a different course; . . . none of you, not even all of you together, have ever known as much grief, suffering, and humiliation as I have! . . . But – life is beautiful!'[5]

Here, witting or unwitting, is the joyful spirit of socialist realism. Gorky's mood was not always so euphoric. His pseudonym means 'bitter' in Russian, and he found no difficulty in complaining not only against the vanity and hypocrisy of bourgeois life, in America as well as in Russia, but also the stubborn ignorance of the peasant and proletarian existence. At his best he can be lyrical on both people and things, including the mighty Volga along which he spent much of his early roaming life. Mutual affection for a river as well as the choice of a pseudonym link A. M. Peshkov with S. L. Clements, that is, Gorky with Twain. Both could be called the first writers in their respective societies from the people and for the people, and both were journalists as well as writers of fiction.

In this last respect they were similar to many other writers in the two great powers, particularly in the U.S.A. Although there were over 2,000 periodicals published in 1912 in nearly 250 Russian towns, the Russian reading public could still not compare with the American, which had developed a voracious appetite for all kinds of ephemeral literature. Believing that their popularity brought responsibility as well as power, many journalists in America at the end of the nineteenth century turned towards muck-raking activities of various kinds, including the portrayal of the injustices and deprivations of both rural and urban life in a new wave of realist fiction. Garland, Crane, Norris, London and Dreiser – there were many of these writers. Some of them dealt not only with the ills induced by the contemporary environment at home, but were called by the wild of the Alaskan frontier, as was Jack London, or captured by the allure of world travel, as was Frank Norris. They also sometimes tried to re-create the past imaginatively. The supreme example of this exercise was Crane's *The Red Badge of Courage*, a novel worthy of comparison with Tolstoy's *War and Peace*, although on a much smaller scale. The confusion of Henry Fleming in the tumult and chaos of battle is reminiscent of that of Pierre Bezukhov at Borodino.

Through war and peace, America and Russia had expanded by the beginning of the twentieth century into great imperialist powers. America had managed to maintain her stability at the same time, although the Populist and Progressive movements demonstrated that the expansion had not been a completely smooth experience. For Tsarist Russia, the imperialist experience was too much. She embarked upon the related process of industrial modernisation too late and from too unstable a base for her to be able to survive the climax of the imperialist era, the First World War.

Although increasingly fearful for their continued prosperity, the supporters of Tsarism continued to assert boldly the rightness of Russia's imperialist mission. Even after Tsarism's fall, the Provisional Government's Foreign Minister, Miliukov, talked a similar language of national objectives and interests until his resignation, although adding words to it from the vocabulary of democracy that he may partly have learned in the United States. There it had certainly been possible to talk at the same time of expansion and liberalism. The Progressives experienced little difficulty in simultaneously supporting reform at home and expansion abroad. Their platform of 1912 declared, 'It is imperative to the welfare of our people that we enlarge and extend our foreign commerce. In every way possible our federal government should co-operate in this important matter.' In 1916 their National Committee condemned the government for its failure 'to deal adequately with National honor and industrial welfare', and complained that 'the Wilson administration has repudiated the faith of our forefathers which made the American flag the sufficient protection of an American citizen around the world'.[6] Perhaps their criticism contributed to the conversion of the President; certainly, there was no preacher like that convert.

6 The Age of the Proletarian Revolution, 1917-1941

Every century in modern times has had a country to which it looked as what might be called its 'conscience-model'. England was to Voltaire and the Encyclopaedists in the eighteenth century the land of liberties, peace, Isaac Newton and the Quakers. France during the nineteenth century held Europe's revolutionary beacon. The Soviet Union during the fifteen years after the October Revolution became the conscience-model of the world's intellectuals.[1]

So writes Lewis S. Feuer in an article on American travellers to the Soviet Union in the years 1917-32, and the contribution of their impressions to the formation of the ideology of the New Deal. To a declining extent perhaps, with the rise of Nazism and the international crisis, his remarks are still relevant for the period down to 1941, National Socialism being an ugly distortion of the Marxist message and the international crisis, notably in Spain but also throughout Europe and Asia, being closely linked to the events of 1917 in Russia. Just as the eighteenth-century democratic revolution might be said, then, to have exerted a profound influence from the Atlantic to the Urals, a proletarian revolution of the twentieth century can be considered to have made an impact on a wider, even world-wide scale.[2]

It all began in March 1917, when Russia showed that she was still somewhat out of step with the West by undergoing her February Revolution; after three hundred years of existence, the Romanov dynasty fell. Strictly speaking, of course, the monarchy rather faded away, for when Nicholas II abdicated, his brother the Grand Duke Michael agreed to take the crown in his place, but only if it were offered him by a popularly elected Constituent Assembly, thus echoing in a modern manner the election of Michael, the first Romanov, by an earlier form of national assembly in February 1613. In September, Kerensky's government used whatever authority it still possessed to declare Russia a republic. The lingering nature of the death of the monarchy was of more than anecdotal importance, since it revealed something essential to an understanding of its successor, the Provisional Government. Not only did this group of Duma politicians look forward, like the Grand Duke Michael, to a Constituent Assembly for a future sanction of their administration; they also looked backwards to their careers under Tsarism as a sanction for their assumption of power after the abdication. Theirs were the top hats and frock coats of all respectable middle-class politicians of the time.

Very soon they were to find their position threatened, partly by the chaos endemic in war and revolution, partly by a rival organisation, the Soviet of Workers' and Soldiers' Deputies. The Soviet contained professional politicians as well as some workers and soldiers, but few of them had been in the Duma; more had been in exile. The Soviet was to the left of the Provisional Government, then, although it would be true to say that it was to the right of the people in its readiness to compromise with the Duma ministers. The people were for peace, for land, for bread; even the Bolsheviks did not come out unequivocally for these three basic wants until after the celebrated arrival in April at the Finland Station of their leader, Lenin. By popular demand, the Provisional Government jettisoned some of its bourgeois ministers in May, and Kerensky, an embodiment of the uneasy relations between it and the Soviet, moved into the ascendancy. Although the Bolsheviks were driven into retreat by the failure of the workers and soldiers, still more radical than Lenin and his associates, to drive out Kerensky and his men in the July days, the abortive Kornilov coup showed by early September that counter-revolution from the right was an empty threat, that there was no danger in the Bolsheviks moving to throw out the isolated Kerensky. The Soviets were becoming Bolshevik, and popular sovereignty could be declared in the cry for all power to them.

Even Kerensky had attempted to appeal to popular sovereignty rather than to the residue of monarchical legitimacy as he declared Russia a republic in September and hastened to convene the Constituent Assembly, which had previously been put off for a series of reasons, largely connected with the continuance of the war. It had been argued, perfectly reasonably if the war were accepted as a basic premise, that conditions of national emergency were incompatible with the summons of such a body. But as Kerensky was drowning in a sea of anarchy, he clutched at the straw of the Constituent Assembly to save him. Conversely, the Bolsheviks under Lenin, who had been pressing for the convocation of the Constituent Assembly before October, were strong enough after their revolution to dismiss it contemptuously as soon as it had met. The Bolsheviks, probably to their surprise, had received a minority of the votes cast in elections to the Constituent Assembly, but Lenin argued that such results were meaningless in comparison with the seizure of power in October. The vanguard of the revolutionary movement, the urban proletariat, through the agency of the Soviets and under the guidance of the Bolsheviks, had dismissed Kerensky, and now, entering into alliance with the poorest ranks of the peasantry, would eliminate the influence of bourgeois, petit-bourgeois and other class enemies to give Lenin's government the most genuinely popular support a government had ever enjoyed in Russia or anywhere else in the world.

Accept this argument, and everything else follows. The imperialist war should not be continued, but the revolution must be vigorously defended against the Whites and the American and other interventionists. The old pre-revolutionary army was an instrument of class oppression, but the new Red Army was the weapon of the people. The land should be taken from the landlords and the kulaks, and then the peasants would come to want to join collectives. Similarly, with the factory-owners dispossessed, the workers would co-operate in fraternal control of industry. The national minorities, many of which had wanted to separate from imperialist Great Russia, would enter into close alliance with the socialist Russian republic, once the chains of Tsarist oppression had been broken. World revolution, although still the ultimate aim of the Communist Party, had to be put off indefinitely after the Communists had been forced to agree to a proletarian Tilsit peace at Brest-Litovsk. Similarly, circumstances soon forced Lenin to compromise at home, to take one step back in preparation for two steps forward. Peasant and worker opposition had revealed that the weight of history acted like a brake on revolutionary progress, that conditions were not yet mature enough for the transition to socialism to be immediate, and so the concessions of the New Economic Policy, a peasant Brest-Litovsk, were introduced. But sight was not lost of the ultimate aim. World revolution and Communism were still the ends which justified such means as N.E.P. The New Economic Policy did not work all that smoothly, however, and Lenin's physical breakdown may have been brought on partly by his realisation that to gain power, a difficult enough task to which he had devoted all his adult life, had been easier than to use it as had been hoped, to bring Communism to Russia and to the world.

Similarly, Woodrow Wilson met with a crippling nemesis of power in his attempt to persuade his fellow Americans to share the vision of a world kept safe for democracy and immune from Communism through the full participation of the United States in the League of Nations. His successor, Warren G. Harding, called for a return to normalcy, which meant for him playing cards with his home-town cronies in the White House, and for many of those who voted for him a return to the good old days of isolationism and *laissez-faire* before the war, even those before the twentieth century. The other two presidents of the 1920s, Harding's fellow Republicans, Coolidge and Hoover, looked at American domestic policies in a similar *laissez-faire* manner. Yet while on the whole wishing to bid a firm farewell to Wilsonian and war controls, the administrations of the 1920s saw the advantages of retaining some aspects of them. Planning and integration of the economy with government supervision and encouragement had been good for business as well as for the U.S.A. Price-fixing, monopoly, direction of labour had all played their part here, and were to continue to do so, even though they clashed with the philosophy of freedom, and in some cases were characteristic of socialism, or at least state capitalism. The direction later given by the New Deal was not completely new, then, but rather took the trend of the 1920s a stage further.

Moreover throughout American history the paradox had existed of an official declaration of a *laissez-faire* policy on the one hand and the implementation of something very different on the other. It is not necessary to be an unregenerate disciple of Beard to discern this constant theme. Land and business interests undoubtedly influenced the government in the early years of the Republic's development, and gained considerable assistance from administrations proclaiming that it was their duty to interfere as little as possible with the economy and all other aspects of the national life. Then, after the Civil War during the age of the Robber Barons, politicians had been proclaiming freedom and equality at the same time as handing out money and land to railroad men and other entrepreneurs. As then, so in the 1920s, the system was clearly shown up for what it was only when carried to excess. It needed the revelation of the Crédit Mobilier operation and other such swindles to lay bare the essential meaning of the Gilded Age. And now a darker side to normalcy was uncovered by the publicity given to scandals in government departments, some of which revealed collusion between members of the administration and oil interests and are said to have hastened Harding's premature death. Coolidge presented the complete picture of cool probity; the system, however, continued through his presidency to the beginning of that of the unimpeachable Hoover.

In 1929 the paradoxical system resolved its contradictions in the Great Crash. Whatever poor Hoover did, his political career was finished, and Franklin D. Roosevelt virtually became president by winning the Democratic nomination. The New Deal took the trend inaugurated by the First World War and adumbrated in the decades before it several stages further. Not only did the government give hand-outs to business, however, it also spared a few dimes for workers and farmers, encouraged the growth of unions and erected a framework, albeit rather scanty, for social welfare. This was already enough to raise the cry of Communism among F.D.R.'s opponents, but the New Deal went further still in the bold experiment of conservation and electrification, T.V.A. Here was planning and federal action on a large scale indeed. Opposition to the measure was correspondingly great, and similar schemes for other river valleys were not developed.

For at least three reasons, however, the New Deal could not be said to have introduced into the United States a socialist revolution. In the first place it bolstered up the capitalist economy rather than overthrew it. To quote Morison and Commager:

> Historically Franklin Roosevelt's administration did for twentieth-century American capitalism what Theodore Roosevelt's and Wilson's had done for nineteenth-century business enterprise: it saved the system by ridding it of its grosser abuses and forcing it to accommodate itself to larger public interests. History may eventually record Franklin D. Roosevelt as the greatest American conservative since Hamilton.[3]

Secondly, a peaceful socialist revolution was an impossibility; it took some courage and determination on F.D.R.'s part even to carry the New Deal as far as he did. The executive found itself checked and balanced by both the legislative and judicial branches of government, as well as by respectable business opinion. Thirdly, the problems introduced by the Great Depression had by no means been solved completely, let alone in a revolutionary manner, when a boom was injected into the economy by the onset of the Second World War rather than by domestic pump-priming.

Between the wars the attention of the Soviet Union, like that of the United States, was mainly directed inwards. Wilson's dream of enthusiastic American participation in the League of Nations was shattered, as was Lenin's of the peoples of the Soviet Union quickly accompanying those of all other nations through world revolution. (Broken partly by the failure of their dreams, they died within a few days of each other.) The idea of socialism in one country was launched at least as early as that of the New Economic Policy. Progress towards socialism, declared Lenin, was dependent on either world revolution or a compromise with the domestic peasant majority. N.E.P. was a recognition of the necessity of choosing the second of the two alternatives. But this choice did not mean the end of the debate; the nature, extent and duration of the compromise with the peasantry provided fuel for controversy among the members of the Communist Party throughout the 1920s. At one extreme there were those who wished the Soviet Union to progress towards industrialisation, the basis for socialism, with the steps of a tortoise. Encouragement of the middle and lower peasants, if not the kulaks, to enrich themselves would provide in the not too distant future the capital necessary for the industrialisation. This great transformation would then take place with the minimum of social dislocation. At the other extreme, the left group in the debate, without suggesting emulation of the hare of the fable, of course, were for rapid change in a world of permanent revolution. The city and the factory must arrive in the U.S.S.R. quickly, partly because this would be the least painful way, all things considered; partly because the opposition of the capitalist powers to the Soviet Union demanded it; and partly because the New Economic Policy was not working. The scissors crisis, a phenomenon isolated by Trotsky, revealed the inability of town and country to compromise as the peasants sold their abundant produce, and then became reluctant to sell it, at prices low in comparison to those asked for the relatively scarce industrial goods.

Trotsky's analysis prevailed, but Trotsky himself was exiled. Trotsky, a brilliant if sometimes wayward thinker but not a clever politician, was outmanœuvred by Stalin, a comparatively pedestrian theoretician but a skilful manipulator of men and exploiter of opportunities. The struggle between the two giants, it must be remembered, was a reflection of a combat between conflicting issues at all levels of the party. Stalin, as General Secretary, was able to be at once in tune with the feeling of the rank-and-file and the N.C.O.s of the C.P.S.U. and to manipulate that feeling. This explains his shifts of ideological position in the 1920s, his borrowings from the arguments of others, including Trotsky's.

From the big debate of the 1920s Soviet politics moved into the crushing unanimity of the late 1930s. The cult of personality made its entrance, and all its opponents, real and imagined, came to an unpleasant end. Again, however, it is an over-simplification, and one over-indulged in by Marxists who should know better, to discuss the 1930s in terms of Stalin alone. While it cannot be denied that the small Georgian was larger than life and struck terror and reverence by turns into Soviet hearts, he, like the other so-called great men of history, was much more at the mercy of circumstances than a moulder of them. The great turmoil of the first five-year plans, the growing world crisis, the move from mass illiteracy to mass literacy, to mention just three aspects of the situation, moulded the proletariat's leader as much as Nicholas had been powerless in the face of similar troubles at a much earlier stage at the beginning of the twentieth century.

Stalin does not make a very great appearance in recent Soviet history books, in contrast with those written during his later lifetime, when barely a page could go by without some mention of him. Undoubtedly the truth of his influence is nearer the first extreme than the second, as has just been argued, but it is difficult to accept without reservation such statements as the following, taken from a recently published short history of the U.S.S.R. and concerning the introduction in the 1930s of a new constitution to replace that of 1924:

A decision to draft a new Constitution was passed at the Seventh All-Union Congress of Soviets in 1935. In 1936, it was published in the press for nation-wide discussion.

Nearly half the adult population took part in the discussion.

The new Constitution was adopted in November 1936 by the Eighth Extraordinary Congress of Soviets of the U.S.S.R. in Moscow.

It recorded the triumph of socialism and provided the foundation for broad socialist democracy, stating that a socialist economic system and ownership of the means of production were the economic basis of the Soviet Union, while the Soviets of Working People's Deputies were its political foundation. It removed the remaining restrictions in elections to the Soviets, replaced multi-stage elections by direct elections and established the election of all Soviets on the basis of universal, equal and direct suffrage by secret ballot. Citizens of the U.S.S.R. received equal rights to elect and be elected to the Soviets.[4]

Obviously this is a somewhat idealised picture. Nevertheless it is wrong to look on all meetings during the period as nothing more than rubber-stamp propaganda rallies. Up to the middle 1930s at least, arguments could be quite wide and genuine on problems facing a factory or a farm. The proletarian revolution had indeed marked a step forward in the political consciousness of the Soviet peoples.

In contrast with the democratic revolution, which had come to an end with a great international conference at Vienna, the proletarian revolution's beginning was marked by such a congress, this time at Versailles. On both occasions the assembled powers were most interested in the maintenance of stability and the *status quo ante bellum*, but on the former occasion Europe's equilibrium had been restored after revolution, on the second just upset by it. As far as the super-powers were concerned, Russia was the major advocate of reaction at Vienna and kept out of Versailles, the U.S.A. was a distant spectator of Vienna and the leading power at Versailles, where it took over the part that Russia had played at the earlier assembly. After Versailles, as we have noted above, America went into its shell, and the U.S.S.R. was beginning to look inwards too. However, although capitalism in one country might have been F.D.R.'s early slogan as much as socialism in one country was Stalin's, complete isolation was not possible for either super-power in the inter-war years, nor did either of them seek it. The banner of world revolution was kept flying by the Third International; less obviously, a world safe for democracy was the tacit aspiration of the American Government throughout the 1920s if not the 1930s.

Thus, while the U.S.A. did not join the League of Nations, it co-operated with the organisation energetically. Under American sponsorship, the great naval nations of the world agreed to limit their expansion proportionately to avoid another arms race in the Washington Treaty of 1922. Over sixty nations, including the U.S.S.R., eventually joined with the U.S.A. and France in the multilateral agreement proposed in 1928 by Secretary of State Kellogg, in which the contracting powers agreed to 'condemn recourse to war for the solution of international controversies, and renounce it as an instrument of national policy'. Pan-Americanism was reoriented for good neighbours rather than big and little brothers. A wary eye was kept on the Pacific, although nothing was done at first to counter Japanese expansionism. The Open Door policy in China was persisted with until Japan slammed it in America's face. In Europe, defeated Germany was given several concessions concerning repayment of her war reparations, and generally bolstered up until she was ready for another attempt at world power.

While America slept throughout the 1930s, other powers were hardly more alert to the growing menace of Fascism in Europe. The Soviet Union, however, where memories of deep German penetration were still fresh, became alarmed at a somewhat earlier stage than her future allies, although its record is not one of consistent awareness of the way Europe was going. This observation must be briefly elaborated. Once the idea of permanent proletarian revolution had been largely replaced by that of socialism in one country, the U.S.S.R.'s foreign policy was at least recognisable as such, and the Third International was made subservient to the needs of socialism's fortress. By 1921 came a trade agreement with Great Britain, and treaties of various kinds with several states. Unlike the U.S.A., the Soviet Union did at last join the League of Nations in 1934, and participated in many of its activities. In 1929 Litvinov echoed the Kellogg proposals with a regional protocol, and in the 1930s continually reiterated the idea of 'collective security', particularly after the rise of Hitler which Soviet miscalculation had done something to promote. Left out of Munich, withdrawing from Spain, the Soviet Union retreated into isolation by the end of 1938, and then made a third Tilsit peace with Germany, which allowed the area still unrecovered from the second, Brest-Litovsk, to be taken back, and some more too. In the Far East also, Soviet diplomacy was active in the inter-war period, the half-hearted nature of its support for Mao and the Communists there sowing some of the seeds of later dissension. Like the U.S.A., the U.S.S.R. did nothing to stop the infiltration of Japan into China.

For such action, lines of communication through Siberia would have been over-extended, and the development of the frontier was largely pre-empting Soviet energies there. New industry was being developed in Siberia, new towns were being built. For example, the young Communists worked on the construction of a new town named after them, Komsomolsk, with hammers, saws and hatchets.

The conditions in which Komsomolsk was born can readily be understood from the following description of them:

> The first winter of 1932–33 was the most fearful of all; not only was there a flood which carried away much of the timber needed for building new houses, but typhus took a heavy toll among the Komsomols, and scurvy was almost general. The nearest town was 250 miles away; there were no vitamins, no medical supplies, and almost no food. The vitamins had to be replaced by a concoction made of pine-needles which tasted horrible. The few peasants in the neighbourhood sold potatoes at fifteen roubles a piece, roughly ten shillings.[5]

While the Soviet frontier was still very wild indeed, the American, it will be recalled, had closed in 1890. There was still some filling-up to do, but with the onset of the Great Depression in 1929 the frontier possibly receded somewhat as it had done during earlier depressions during the nineteenth century. This time, however, it receded to the west as well as to the east, many Okies and Arkies making the great trek to California.

At the end of the Depression the American population had moved slightly from east to west as well as from north to south. The east–west ratio went from 70:30 in 1920 to 69:31 in 1940, while in the same period the north–south proportion moved from 63 minus : 37 plus to 62:38, after a move in the other direction to 63 plus : 37 minus in 1930. For all the dislocation produced by the revolutions of Lenin and Stalin, the distribution of the Soviet population did not alter radically during the period, although Siberia began to fill up rather more quickly than before. In both societies the movement to the city was vigorous, the American rural–urban ratio shifting from 30:70 in 1920 to 23:77 in 1940, while in the U.S.S.R. the percentage of city dwellers increased from 18 in 1926 to 28 in 1939. Generally, the Soviet population increased from 147 million at the first All-Union census of 1926 to 170 million at the second in 1939. For all its expansion in the inter-war period, the Soviet population suffered a deficit of about 32 million between 1914 and 1941, most of this accounted for by the First World War and revolution, and the civil war, famine and epidemics consequent upon them, but no small amount resulting from the upsets produced by the drive towards collectivisation of agriculture and the forced pace of industrialisation. Meanwhile in the U.S.A. the total population increased from 106 million in 1920 to 132 million in 1940; although it suffered far less than the U.S.S.R. during the inter-war period, it did not go very far to making up the population gap between the super two.

The year 1929 marks a watershed in the economic development of both powers in the period under discussion. Although there is less of a sharp break in the American than in the Soviet case, the Great Depression forced the government to take a number of important decisions increasing its own importance in the management of both the economy and society. The Stalin revolution getting under way in 1929 brought radical changes to the lives of all the peoples of the U.S.S.R., although, as has been noted above, the limitations of the great socialist construction can be seen in the circumstance that the population could not be pushed around to produce the optimum balance of human and natural resources.

In agriculture, perhaps the most revolutionary change since the introduction of the plough took place between the wars. This was the substitution of the tractor for the horse, and with it the conquest of the age-long isolation of the farming community with the increased use of the automobile and the truck. In 1918 in the U.S.A., where change was more gradual, there were in use approximately 85,000 tractors, 80,000 trucks and 950,000 automobiles. By 1940 these figures had grown to 1,567,000, 1,047,000, and 4,144,000 respectively. In the U.S.S.R., where comparable totals would have been very small indeed in 1918, they had grown by the end of the first two five-year plans in 1938 to 456,000 tractors, 128,000 combine harvesters, and 146,000 trucks. The Soviet Union obviously lagged behind in the mechanisation of agriculture and in such other revolutionary rural developments as electrification, irrigation, fertilisation and hybridisation. Russia's historic backwardness was still exacting its toll in this and many other spheres of life, and it was not only technical, but cultural and political too. These three elements came together in the M.T.S., the machine-tractor station, a nucleus of progress wherever it was found. The greatest change in Soviet agriculture between the wars, however, was collectivisation. During this process and the accompanying liquidation of the kulaks, there was much distress and error, but the pace was forced relentlessly and over 90 per cent of the peasants were in collectives by the end of the second five-year plan. Meanwhile in America, the basic unit of agricultural production remained the single-family farm, albeit a bigger, more businesslike concern than before 1914. It had to be to survive, and many farmers were forced to give up their way of life during the Depression, as the corporations adopted it.

With the introduction of motor machines and transport, agriculture and industry were divided by a gulf much narrower than that traditionally separating them. In the case of the Soviet Union the connection was made closer by the need to graft industry on to an economy which had experienced something like an industrial revolution in reverse during the revolutionary years. The U.S.A. had long ceased to depend on agriculture to increase the capitalisation of industry; the U.S.S.R., backward and cut off from the world credit system, could get its finance by no other means. During the first critical years after 1917, the so-called policy of War Communism meant little more than the rape of the countryside to ensure the bare survival of a crippled industry and starving towns. From 1921, the New Economic Policy encouraged farmers to produce, to feed the growing urban population and to create capital for industry through export. The N.E.P. was partially successful, but slow. For domestic and foreign reasons, ideological and practical, the pace had to be quickened at the end of the 1920s. Moreover, as the peasants enriched themselves in rural Russia, the industrial sector lagged behind, and there was an excessive imbalance reducing the measure of N.E.P.'s effectiveness.

The U.S.A.'s crisis of 1929, like that of the U.S.S.R., was fundamentally the result of a loss of equilibrium, although at a more advanced stage of economic progress. The Great Depression was a clear example of a fault still to be found today in the American capitalist economy, 'high-level underdevelopment'. America's production and ability to produce in both agriculture and industry had outrun the capacity of her people to consume; F.D.R.'s New Deal was essentially an attempt to bring back balance by reducing production or keeping it under control, while priming the pump, increasing consumption and the capacity to consume.

Although there had been planning in the American economy before, particularly under the impact of the First World War, it was now considerably increased. In this development a leaf or two were taken out of the Soviet book, which itself had been written not only according to Marx and Engels, but also after the experience of Germany, the country most recently undergoing industrialisation before the U.S.S.R., and even a little from pre-revolutionary Russian experience of planning. Pragmatic economists, labour leaders, social workers, politicians and engineers all praised what they had seen during visits to the Soviet Union. It is difficult, even impossible, however, to calculate how much of their enthusiasm was transmitted into the domestic and foreign policies of the U.S.A., although interesting to consider how great the amount could have been. As Lewis S. Feuer writes:

> The American travelers did not have more than their usual share of human naïveté. They saw realities strongly. They did not foresee the latent evil of Stalinism. The Soviet social world turned out to be less determinate and predictable than they thought. Their perception was perspectival, as all perceptions are, but it was not false. And perhaps if their advice had been followed, some evils might have been spared both the Soviet Union and the rest of the world. Perhaps if the United States had earlier abandoned the Hoover theses, if it had welcomed Soviet society into the world's councils, if it had staved off depression by progressive economic measures, perhaps if action had been taken early against Nazi Germany, then a more moderate, right-wing form of Bolshevism might have emerged dominant. We cannot say. But American liberals must understand rather than repress the chapter of Soviet influence from their history of the past.[6]

While speculating about the Soviet impact on America, we should not ignore the American impact on the Soviet Union. Not only did the U.S.A. present a target, albeit a receding one, for the Soviet economy to aim at, it also provided technical assistance, both theoretical and practical. For example, the Taylorian system of time and motion study, piece-rate labour and general scientific management was accepted by the U.S.S.R. after having first been rejected by it, and evolved, partly at least, into 'socialist emulation'. Ford engineers, as Stalin pointed out in 1933, helped create the Soviet automobile industry. Although Ford lost more than half a million dollars on its enterprise in the Soviet Union, his biographers tell us that 'Henry Ford would gladly have sacrificed twice that sum to give his ideas a practical illustration on the world stage'.[7]

By 1941, in the U.S.S.R., heavy industry had been developed to a considerable degree, the industrial workers had grown in number and expertise, agricultural workers reduced in number but collectively organised, and a new intelligentsia formed of managers, administrators and party men. The emergence of the Soviet intelligentsia has been cited as the basis of a bureaucratic degeneration inherent in the working-out of the revolution. If indeed there was some clogging of the governmental wheels, mismanagement and red-tape of one kind or another, this may be seen at least partly as a legacy of pre-revolutionary times. In the more advanced U.S.A., where industrial progress had outrun social, the 1930s brought a huge growth in unionisation and the beginnings of a social security programme. Immigrants revealed in these processes that they were now mature Americans, and ready to play a full part in political and social activity; the Negroes became more organised too.

Internationally, the 1930s were not very constructive from an economic point of view. Leaving the London Conference, F.D.R. refused to let the U.S.A. help solve the difficult problem of international liquidity. The U.S.S.R. had trade agreements with several capitalist nations, but did not enter the complex world financial system. Both super-powers, then, would not shoulder the burden appropriate to their strength in the maintenance of the world's financial stability. The problem of imbalance, which domestically had given the U.S.A. and the U.S.S.R. their greatest economic problems of the inter-war period, was very much more intense on the world scale, and international financial difficulties partly reflected this.

Apart from the economic and social, one of the most profound aspects of the proletarian revolution in the U.S.S.R. was the educational. In 1917 not much more than a third of the Soviet people were literate; by 1926 over a half of them; by 1939 more than four-fifths. Such a great step forward was not taken without considerable difficulty and several significant changes in educational policy. And literacy, important though it is, marks only the beginning of education. So, while struggling to make sure that all children and adults could read and write, Soviet educators were already planning the introduction of universal primary and secondary education. In this endeavour they were hampered by lack of buildings and teachers; it was not until the middle of the 1930s that there were sufficient materials and people for the All-Union coverage of even the four elementary grades. A further problem was the necessity of translating and transliterating Turkic languages, and of creating a written language for some of the backward peoples inhabiting the U.S.S.R. Practical questions such as these were all discussed in conjunction with the theoretical guidance received from Marx and Engels and other sources. The fathers of Communism believed that the harmonious development of children would best be attained by an education that was polytechnical, concerned with the development of technical proficiency, as well as of mind and body. Thus the great divide between blue-collar and white-collar work would be broken down, and everybody equally appreciated for his contribution to society. Lenin basically agreed that education should be polytechnical, but it was not only from the Communist trinity that Soviet educators drew their ideas. For example, they were also interested in another society that had struggled with the obstacle of mass cultural backwardness, the U.S.A., and adapted several of the ideas of progressive education. Cultural cross-currents now became inextricably intermingled. Inspired in the first place to some extent by a Russian exhibit at the Philadelphia Centennial Exhibition, the progressive ideal came over to the Soviet Union, where its implementation gave further encouragement to people such as John Dewey himself. Returning from a visit to the U.S.S.R., the great pragmatist declared in 1928: 'The main effort is nobly heroic, evincing a faith in human nature which is democratic beyond the ambitions of the democracies of the past.' A friend of Dewey's said in 1929 that Soviet Russia had embarked upon 'the outstandingly ambitious enterprise that educational history has to show'.

In America, if there was absent the enthusiastic spirit that can be generated only by revolution, there was tremendous expansion in education during the inter-war years. Over a million young Americans were enjoying secondary education in 1910, it will be remembered. By 1929–30 the figure approached 5 million, and by 1939–40 it was over 7 million. The U.S.A., then, could aspire to universal secondary education, while the U.S.S.R. was still struggling to give primary education to every child. American university attendance was proportionately higher too. Educational administration was rationalised in most of the states, with many school districts being consolidated and the school bus becoming a common feature of rural life. And the ideas launched in the U.S.A. at the turn of the century were still alive and spreading. In 1937 the Committee on Experimental Schools of the Progressive Educational Association wrote:

It is evident ... that the tendency to be avowedly experimental is gaining ground. To 'experiment with children', to 'experiment with taxpayers' money', are not the crimes they used to be. 'Radical notions' may safely be incorporated in the instructions of a city superintendent to his corps of principals and teachers, or in the public pronouncement of a state commissioner concerning his plans for a drastic overhauling of the whole educational machinery of his state. In short, there is growing perception of the truth that a rapidly changing society demands a responsive effort on the part of education; there is a growing public which willingly supports such responses.[8]

A year later, even *Time* magazine could observe that progressive education was no longer a rebel movement; it had become respectable.

This respectability may have been gained in the U.S.A. partly because it had been lost in the U.S.S.R. In 1931 the Central Committee of the Communist Party had brought education back from a broad training for citizenship to a narrower framework of conventional subjects taught in the traditional manner. Discipline and the rote system returned, as did the former oral examinations and five-point scale of grades. The international outlook of the pioneer years was to a considerable extent replaced by a fervent Soviet patriotism, which included the admiration of such historical figures as Alexander Nevsky and Peter the Great.

Such a development was to be found in the world of the arts, for example, in Eisenstein's film of Nevsky and Alexei Tolstoy's novel on Peter. Stalin, even more than Lenin, was a man of simple, traditional tastes, and both their views were very influential. They also reflected the attitudes of many of the Soviet people, who had found it difficult to appreciate some of the works produced in their name in the 1920s. Mayakovsky and others believed that some of the modernist movements of the beginning of the century were adaptable to the needs of the post-revolutionary situation, and were the only part of pre-revolutionary culture that should not be completely abandoned. A thousand cultural flowers bloomed during the N.E.P. period, however, and some writers went so far as to abjure narrow definition of their literary activity. For example, the leader of the group known as the Serapion brothers declared: 'And now when the fanatical politicians and the short-sighted critics of the right or the left wing attempt to sow discord among us, emphasising our divergent ideologies and cry out: "Let every one follow his own party" we only ignore them.' But who were the Serapion brothers to the millions just breaking through to literacy? And what could the workers make of Futurism, which Mayakovsky had declared to be the art of the proletariat? Perhaps the growth of a true socialist culture would take a long time to create.

But the party could not wait for this eventuality, any more than for a tortoise-pace industrialisation. At the beginning of the 1930s it called on writers to subscribe to the theory of 'socialist realism', the literary equivalent of the 'general party line'. The concept of 'socialist realism' evaded exact definition, but was caught by a party directive of 1934 which asked writers 'to express in images the new aspect of the country, the changing mode of life, the new thoughts, feelings and aspirations of the people'. The application of such principles to their novels and stories gave much trouble to the members of the now monolithic Union of Soviet Writers. While celebrating the heroic struggle of the international proletariat, they would have to avoid the extremes of rootless cosmopolitanism. They should not dwell on the darker side of life in the Soviet Union in the 1930s, but at the same time not minimise the difficulties faced in the period of the construction of socialism. It would be no consolation to those who failed to meet these requirements to know that one of their colleagues who had been condemned for such shortcomings, Michael Sholokhov, was to become one of the most celebrated of all Soviet writers. Sholokhov's *And Quiet Flows the Don* certainly ranks as one of the finest books produced in the U.S.S.R. between the wars. Nor can there be denial of the worth of another portrayal of Cossack savage chivalry, Isaac Babel's *Red Cavalry*. Ilf and Petrov celebrated the arrival of the automobile and poked fun at the bureaucracy in *The Golden Calf*. Zoshchenko encouraged people to laugh at their own plight in *The Bathhouse* and other such stories, and skilfully applied his spare staccato prose to an autobiographical novel, *Before Sunrise*. Zamyatin preceded and perhaps surpassed Huxley's *Brave New World* and Orwell's *1984* in his *We*. There can be no doubt that post-revolutionary writing at its best produced works worthy of the great tradition it had to draw on, even though the atmosphere was hardly conducive in the 1920s and 1930s to unfettered literary creation. Soviet censorship could be crueller than Tsarist, but in some shape or form was nevertheless a necessity in the period of rapid and fundamental change through which society was passing.

No writer of any intellectual pretensions, and there are few without them, and perhaps no writer with human sympathy, and they all need that, could ignore the Soviet Union during the age of the proletarian revolution. Even the lost American generation of the 1920s could not completely avoid an attitude towards Marx and Lenin, although Freud was a strong rival for their attention. While the most self-consciously receptive to the spirit of the age failed to produce its best work, John Dos Passos and John Steinbeck nearly do justice to some of its principal themes. (An interesting ironic anecdote concerning the trilogy *U.S.A.* is that Dos Passos is said to have met the prototype for one of its characters, the millionaire J. Ward Moorhouse, in the Hotel Moskva of the Soviet capital. Like Dos Passos, Steinbeck took an interest in the U.S.S.R. and visited it.) Obviously, even Steinbeck and Dos Passos are working in the American traditions of the frontier and the city, as well as being influenced by recent developments in the rest of the world. The voyage of the Okie Joad family to California in their broken-down covered wagon of a malfunctioning truck has with it some of the saga of the earlier westward movement, and *The Grapes of Wrath* is also in the tradition of Twain, with its strong regionalism and the river becoming the road. Dos Passos draws on the realist tradition established before the First World War, although bringing it up to date with, for example, his newsreels interludes, and he shares with the muck-raking novelists of the 1890s a strong fear of the failure of the great American dream.

Hemingway is also in such American traditions, although often attempting to reject them. Man against nature is perhaps his most recurring theme, and more likely to be varied in Cuba or Africa than the American west. He deals too with the problems of war and the boredom of city life, although here the setting is usually European. Most obviously in *For Whom the Bell Tolls*, Hemingway concerns himself with socialism also, although the action takes place in the mountains, and Jordan addresses himself to the bridge rather as other Hemingway heroes face up to a lion. At his best, Hemingway meets the complexities of modern life or the simplicities of nature with a penetrating directness. Another approach to the complicated alienation of the inter-war American existence was an alienated complication of style, achieved most notably by a writer who avoids the big questions of the hour and concentrates on those posed in an archaic backwater. There are not many advocates of proletarian revolution in the Yoknapatawpha County of William Faulkner; on the other hand illuminating examples are to be found there of an American problem that was to grow to enormous size after the Second World War, that of race.

Yoknapatawpha County had its peers in remoteness in the Soviet Union, and many districts which were superior to it in this respect. Undoubtedly, however, the U.S.S.R. that was to enter the Second

World War had changed enormously from the Russian Empire that had succumbed to the First. At enormous cost, and in a ruthless manner, the Soviet Union had completed the modernising task that had broken Tsarism. Socialism, according to the Soviet pattern at least, had been established in one country, although the effort necessary for this had meant the comparative neglect of Lenin's wider declared purpose, the establishment of socialism throughout the world. The U.S.A., experiencing internal problems of a less serious nature at a higher level of development, moved away in the inter-war years from Wilson's aspiration of a world made safe by America for democracy. For the Soviet Union and the United States, the years of the proletarian revolution were a preparation for their transition from imperialism to super-power.

7 From World Power into Space, 1941–1969

Before the Second World War neither the U.S.A. nor the U.S.S.R. was ready to exert super-power on a world scale. At the end of the war both had no choice; super-power was almost as much thrust on them as sought after. By 1969 their might was being exerted in space as well as on earth, and the moon was within their grasp; a new era of human history was about to begin if they could stop their rivalry from becoming mutually destructive. While this most recent period is the most exciting for a historian to consider, it is also the most difficult for him, for several reasons. Firstly, because of its living reality, he cannot look at it as dispassionately as he can at earlier periods. Secondly, because of its proximity, he can place its events and developments only in a limited perspective. Thirdly, he is confronted with too much evidence concerning some questions such as social and economic development, and impeded by an insufficiency of evidence on other questions such as important political decisions. Turning for assistance to the work of social scientists, who have given this period more of their attention than any other, he finds that they too are hampered by problems of bias and focus. Nevertheless they make the almost impossible task of discussing the culmination of the emergence of the super-powers in an historical manner somewhat less burdensome than it would otherwise be. Another, minor means of working towards this elusive end is to retain the pattern of earlier chapters, considering the period first in a broad sweep and then in a narrower fashion.

The U.S.A. and the U.S.S.R. entered the Second World War in 1941. Both of them knew that they would do so, and were preparing for the eventuality, but neither was completely ready for the attack which brought them into the conflict. Compared to the Soviet Union, the United States had an easy war. The Russian fatherland was deeply penetrated, while the western hemisphere was barely scratched. About 20 million Soviet citizens died, many of them civilians; under half a million Americans, nearly all combatants. The

Russian economy suffered a fearful dislocation, the American moved on from the partial recovery of the New Deal to a great boom.

The two great powers had been too mistrustful of each other before the war to be good allies during it. Although America gave Russia a large amount of aid to keep the eastern front going in Europe, Russia complained bitterly that the western front should have been opened long before it was. Differences of opinion led to an intensified mutual suspicion at important conferences which took place towards the end of the war. While concentrating on the imposition of unconditional surrender on the Axis, the two were coming to realise that they would be the post-war super-powers and moving beyond unconditional surrender towards a division of the power which the victors would necessarily hold. But this could not be done amicably, and the tension increased when the Soviet Union made its late entry into the Pacific War with the express intention of making up the losses incurred by the Tsarist empire in 1905. America's use of the atom bomb in 1945 gave a terrible warning at the end of the Second World War of the probable nature of a third.

Neither power can be blamed exclusively for the Cold War, recent attributions of guilt to the U.S.A. by American academics [1] being as basically misplaced in their well-documented chivalry as the condemnation of the Soviet Union by most of their fellow citizens errs fundamentally in its ignorant slander. The circumstances making for the Cold War were bigger than both of them, and each was at the mercy of its own past and of its ignorance of the past of the other. In the decades following 1945, great crises took the two several times to the brink of war. The nearest approach to it, the Cuban crisis of 1962, fortunately resulted in a greater effort towards communication and mutual understanding. With the emergence of the third world, the Chinese revolution and split with Russia, and the growth of European unity, the dual power of the super two experienced a certain diminution, but there was no serious challenge to it before 1969. Their armed might, their participation in the space race, continued to place them in a category unprecedented and unapproached.

Although the U.S.S.R. entered space first in the person of the late Colonel Gagarin, the U.S.A. had more than caught up by mid-1969 with the trip to the moon of Armstrong, Aldrin and Collins, and continued to lead the way in most other fields. Thus, while both powers were faced by huge problems on the domestic front as well as international difficulties, America's tended to be at a more advanced level.

Soviet agriculture still produced too little and with wide fluctuations from year to year; American farmers still had to be restrained annually from producing too much. The U.S.S.R. found it difficult to embark upon the development of a consumer economy; the U.S.A. to avoid being consumed by it. The world's second super-power was in many ways an underdeveloped country at a time when the richest country in the world had a poverty problem involving people who would be quite prosperous in comparison with most other human beings as well as a few who would not. Just after the Soviet Union had achieved mass literacy, the United States approached mass secondary education. A new electronic culture exerted more influence in America than in Russia. On the other hand the problems of high-level underdevelopment experienced by the affluent society were no less great than those faced by the comparatively poor rival society attempting to overtake it. In our final year of 1969 no domestic conflict appeared to threaten the stability of the Soviet Union as much as the problem of race jeopardised that of the United States.[2]

As we leave the general picture of the most recent period of our history for the detail, the first point to make is that the Second World War was a mighty accelerator of the emergence of the super-powers, just as the First World War had given a tremendous impetus to the proletarian revolution and to American might. In 1941 the world situation had not radically altered since 1918. Two nations, Germany and Japan, had brought the world to war again because they could not accept the continuance of the Versailles settlement. Germany could not indefinitely put up with the loss of her empire and her national pride; Japan discovered that her expansion was too great and too fast for it to be contained peacefully by the other victorious imperialists. And then the acceptance by the other powers of their first aggressive moves, Germany into the Rhineland, Austria and Czechoslovakia, Japan into Manchuria and north China, encouraged them to strive for more. The super two managed to avoid the war at its outbreak, but the launching of Plan Barbarossa in June 1941, and the attack on Pearl Harbor in December of that year, gave them no alternative but to join it. Both the German attack on the U.S.S.R. and the Japanese bombardment of the American fleet appear in retrospect to have involved at least carelessness and perhaps something worse on the part of the Soviet and American leadership, and they have both been sources of bitter historical controversy.[2]

An early strategic decision taken by the Allies was to concentrate on the European theatre of war and to make the Asiatic theatre subordinate to it in importance. While Japan went into south-east Asia and across the Pacific, most of the combined strength of the U.K., the U.S.A. and the U.S.S.R. was turned on Hitler and his allies in North Africa and Europe's eastern extremity. Although the Axis powers continued to advance for a time, by early 1943 the tide had turned with the victory at Guadalcanal in the Solomon Islands, the consolidation of Allied strength in North Africa and the Mediterranean, the successful conclusion to the epic battle of Stalingrad, the commencement of heavy air attacks on Germany and the seizure of superiority over the U-boats in the Atlantic. If not the beginning of the end, this does seem now to have been more than the end of the beginning. Of course, the second front still had to be opened up in Europe, Nazi troops pushed back painfully from Stalingrad to Berlin, and the Japanese expelled from Burma and the Philippines. The Allies still had to show in attacks on German and Japanese cities that they could match the Axis in barbarity.

Meanwhile, in a series of conferences culminating at Yalta, the Allies met to discuss the way the war should be fought and the peace established. Yalta has been a name of infamy to some American historians, the agreements made there by Roosevelt having been seen by them as the last infirmity of a never very noble mind, with F.D.R. carried away by a wild enthusiasm far surpassing that of Wilson at Versailles. In fact Roosevelt was not deserted by his pragmatic sense at Yalta, even though visited by a certain idealism. Thus on the one hand there was the creation of the United Nations Organisation, on the other, already the thought of moving beyond the Atlantic Charter towards NATO. At the same time as working for a lasting peace, F.D.R. was making this difficult to achieve by making agreements which excluded the Soviet Union both from the European and Pacific regions. No wonder that, coming towards victory without an ally on which he could rely, Stalin was at least as keen to establish control over eastern Europe as the U.S.A. was over western. Roosevelt by this time could do little about the split of Europe into spheres of influence, for which Churchill had already been making provision, so he certainly did not give eastern Europe away as some critics have alleged. Not only this; conceding separate votes in the General Assembly of UNO to White Russia and the Ukraine, Roosevelt was no doubt consoled by the continued relevance of his argument in favour of the U.S.A.'s entry into the League of Nations in 1920, that the votes of her Latin American clients would ensure a position of preponderant power in the international organisation. At the time of the Yalta conference, then, Roosevelt, whose ideology was not much clearer than the muddled universalism of Wilson, was making sure that American interests would be protected throughout the world, while Stalin, who still sometimes spoke the clear Leninist language of global revolution, could do no more than try to guarantee the security of the Soviet Union by moving into areas contiguous to it.

During the late 1940s American bases were established in all continents; Soviet armed might was confined to eastern Europe and northern Asia. For a time it seemed that the Soviet Union was making a client of Communist China, but then China broke away in the late 1950s. Meanwhile both super-powers had resorted to force to maintain the spheres of influence which they chose to call theirs, the U.S.S.R. in Hungary, the U.S.A. in Korea. The two had nearly come to war over 'border' incidents, mostly in Berlin. The United Nations Organisation had served largely as a propaganda weapon for the super two, particularly for the United States, since there is much truth in the statement made in the mid-1960s by a Brazilian journalist that the 'U.N. is not an international body but rather a dependency of the U.S. that has been in recent years infiltrated by the Afro-Asians'.[3] Developments within UNO revealed as clearly as the Bandung and other conferences that, having overthrown colonialism, the new nations had no desire to submit to neo-colonialism exerted by either super-power. Both the U.S.A. and the U.S.S.R. found it difficult to adapt to the avowed intentions of the members of the third world, for each was to a certain extent correct in calling the other imperialist, even though the world situation had now become complicated beyond traditional definitions of imperialism and colonialism. America's continued intervention in Vietnam, Russia's in Czechoslovakia, clearly showed in 1969 that the two were finding it no easy task to make allowances for centrifugal forces in the areas which they had come to consider theirs since 1945.

It would perhaps be wrong to leave the international scene without noting that, for all its faults, the United Nations Organisation has more solid achievement to its credit than the League of Nations, although many of its peace-keeping operations have delayed crises rather than solved them. More certainly, the Declaration of Human Rights, containing many of the highest aspirations of both the democratic and proletarian revolutions, commits UNO to aims nobler than those pursued by the League. No less certainly, if these aims are to be less imperfectly realised, the U.S.A. and U.S.S.R. will have to participate in UNO's activities in the most vigorous manner.

Simultaneously with their attempt to keep pace with a rapidly changing international scene and to avert the catastrophe which their possession of terrible new weapons had made probable, the super-powers had to tackle domestic problems of great complexity. Some of these were connected with demobilisation and readjustment at the end of the war, many with the development of industrialised society which the war had accelerated. In purely political terms the years of Truman, Eisenhower, Kennedy and Johnson might not appear to have much in common with those of Stalin, Khrushchev, Brezhnev and Kosygin, yet certain areas of comparability can be discerned nevertheless.

The most important question is that of survival. Have the super-powers found the experience of their emergence an almost unbearable strain on their political cohesion? Will Soviet socialism bury American capitalism, or American democracy sink Russian totalitarianism? In whoever's terms the question is posed, the answer at the end of 1969 is in the negative. In fact this is a comforting thought for both the U.S.S.R. and the U.S.A. since neither would welcome the upset to the world's equilibrium that would result from the collapse of the other. At the same time threats to the stability of both have been apparent enough in the last two decades or so. The U.S.A., although publicly most concerned with the attack from the extreme left, has been subject in fact to a deeper threat from the radical right. Even Eisenhower, a 'pinko' to some observers but right of centre to most, warned against the increasing strength of the military-industrial complex, which cannot have lessened during the succeeding years of the Vietnam war. The apparent ease with which President Truman suppressed General MacArthur does not mean that such confrontations would always result in victory for the civilian commander-in-chief of the armed forces. Possibly, then, the Caesars will come to the United States, as has been somewhat fancifully forecast.[4] In Moscow, on the other hand, where Ivan the Terrible said that the Third Rome would not fall, it could be argued that he was correct in his declaration and it has not fallen; that Stalin was as much a Caesar as his predecessors, and the process of de-Stalinisation is by no means complete; that, if a military-industrial complex is a threat to the United States, a military-bureaucratic establishment exerts control in the Soviet Union as much as something of the same sort did in pre-revolutionary Russia. On the other hand the fall of Zhukov, an interesting parallel to that of MacArthur,[5] appears to testify that the civilian party chiefs are not at the mercy of the generals in the U.S.S.R.

A second menace to the political integrity of the two is that of disintegration through intense pressure from internal unrest. Most obviously, American order has been put to the test by the overlapping urban and race problems. Neither of these is a likely source of upset to Soviet stability at the present time, although there have been some riots in Russian cities and tension between whites and blacks in them. A more powerful centrifugal force operating on the U.S.S.R. is that of nationalism. Nobody would any longer seriously suggest that new states like Alaska or Hawaii or old states like Alabama or Massachusetts would attempt to secede from the Federal Union, but several observers have put forward the opinion that the Central Asian republics or the Ukraine might try to leave the Soviet Union. Fear of the latter breakaway is said to have contributed to the decision to invade Czechoslovakia. The invasion certainly demonstrated how difficult such secession would be. Moreover the trend of the past three hundred years or so appears to be in the direction of making it generally less feasible.

A further danger to the two political systems is their possible obsolescence. Increasingly caught up in bureaucratic paralysis, the argument has been put, they move towards a crippling totalitarianism. Such a tendency has been observed and lamented from left and right, by, for example, Herbert Marcuse and George Wallace. But bureaucracy, like imperialism, capitalism and communism, is an emotionally loaded word; as management and control, it is an inevitable concomitant of advanced civilisation, and cannot be eradicated, either in the Soviet Union, where its development has taken place over a long period, or in the United States, where its origins have been more recent. Another, more dangerous source of obsolescence is acute fear of adaptation and change, revealed to some extent during the dark days of the Cold War by McCarthyism and the Zhdanovshchina. Rigid conformity such as demanded by these two movements could lead only to acute stagnation, particularly the second of them, which was much the more serious and based on the more lamentable tradition. Obsolescence may also be discerned in both basic political structures. According to an article written just before the 1968 presidential election by Professor Commager, the United States commenced its existence as 'the most democratic of political systems', but has since degenerated into 'one of the least democratic'. Commager writes, 'It is sobering, but not surprising, that of the 60 odd nations that have come into existence since 1945 not one has adopted the American form of government'. He refers to political organisations and mechanical contrivances 'all designed to achieve much the same objective: to provide an endless series of appeals, to slow up decisions, and permit minorities to impose their will on majorities'.[6] Thus, pressing domestic and foreign problems, particularly race and Vietnam, could not be dealt with effectively because of obstructionism. As for the Soviet Union, the observer attempting objectivity has to make his way through savage denigration on the one hand and foolish self-congratulation on the other to the assertion that the centralist party control which was certainly necessary in the years after the revolution degenerated during the years of Stalinism and has not yet recovered effectiveness. Nevertheless both American and Soviet government still work in the face of the tremendous problems confronting their super-power, problems little more dreamt of by Lenin than by Washington, so rapid has been the process of its emergence. It may be that both systems are more flexible than their critics charge.

Questions like these can probably be considered more meaningfully in the context of the economic and cultural changes experienced by the U.S.A. and the U.S.S.R. since the 1940s. These after all are the principal factors determining the problems of government. To start with demographic trends, a comparison of the population of the super two made at the end of the 1950s[7] demonstrated that in this respect they were much more similar to each other in size and composition than before the Second World War. Owing largely to the war, the Soviet Union's lead in population was cut from 46 to 18 per cent, with the totals standing at nearly 209 million to America's 177 million. This represents a gain in the United States of more than 35 per cent since 1939, and in the Soviet Union of 9½ per cent. Not all the increase has been natural. As Dr Kantner points out, the U.S.S.R. has acquired about 20 million people through annexation since 1939, approximately as many as the U.S.A. acquired through immigration in the forty years leading up to the imposition of restrictions in 1924. Since the war American immigration has proceeded at a rate fluctuating between 150,000 and 350,000 per annum, while there have been very few immigrants into the Soviet Union.

Natural increase rates were converging by 1957 as well as the population totals, 17·5 per thousand in the Soviet case as opposed to 15·7 per thousand in the American. The rise in the natural growth rates that these figures represent comes from different sources: in the U.S.S.R., from a fall in death rate largely due to improvements in medicine; in the U.S.A., from a rise in birth rate due to affluence. The rates of the super two are more than double those of western Europe, but considerably lower than those of many developing countries in Asia and Africa.

Two pronounced trends emerged between 1939 and 1959 in the geographical redistribution of the Soviet population, to the east and to the city. These mirrored established but continuing trends in American redistribution, to the city and to the west. The convergence that these trends brought about can best be indicated by adapting two tables constructed by Dr Kantner. Firstly, percentage distribution of the area of the U.S.S.R. and its population in 1939 and 1959:

Region	Area	Total		Urban		Rural	
		1939	1959	1939	1959	1939	1959
West of the Urals	21	75·5	69·8	76·1	68·6	75·2	70·9
The Urals and the east	78·9	24·5	30·2	23·9	31·4	24·8	29·1

Secondly, percentage distribution of the area of the U.S.A. and its population in 1940 and 1950:

Region	Area	Total		Urban		Rural	
		1940	1950	1940	1950	1940	1950
East of the Mississippi	29·1	69·2	67·0	74·0	70·4	63·1	64·6
West of the Mississippi	70·9	30·8	33·0	26·0	29·6	36·9	35·4

If the region to the west of the Urals is compared to the region east of the Mississippi and the Soviet east is compared to the American region west of the Mississippi, there are obviously similarities in the percentage population distribution of the U.S.A. and the U.S.S.R. during the most recent period of their history. However, some reservations need to be made to this appearance of convergence. Proportionately more Soviet rural inhabitants are agricultural in their way of life, while their number falls at a time when the number of American rural inhabitants rises. The U.S.A. has fewer cities with populations exceeding totals of 50,000 and 500,000 than the U.S.S.R., but a much greater metropolitan population. American city dwellers are about two-thirds, their Soviet counterparts something more than a half, of their respective total populations. The proportion of males to females is smaller in Soviet Russia for all age groups over 25; the American population lags behind most conspicuously in the pre-school and young adult age groups. Even the pattern of migration is not as uniform as the percentages given above suggest. There are important cross-currents, such as the American drift from the rural south, the industrial east, the farming regions of the Middle West and the mountainous Appalachians and Ozarks. For their part the Russian people have moved in significant numbers to the Baltic provinces as well as to Siberia. A migratory phenomenon exclusive to the U.S.A. is reflected in the forecast that 60 per cent of black Americans will be living in the north by 1975 as compared to 20 per cent in 1920. Roughly a tenth of all Americans are black. Great Russians were about a half of the Soviet people in the late 1950s; their nearest American equivalent, the white Protestants, were something more than half of the U.S.A.'s total.

The social significance of some of these statistics will be referred to briefly below, after a short survey has been made of economic developments during the period under discussion. The agricultural sector indicated very clearly problems that faced the economies more widely, Soviet farming continually facing the problem of under-production, American farming that of overproduction. This was a reflection of comparative Soviet backwardness, for while the area of cultivation and the agricultural labour force were greater in the U.S.S.R., the U.S.A.'s production was superior per acre, per man and overall. The gap was largely due to the far greater use of machinery and fertiliser in the U.S.A., which had at its disposal four times as many trucks and tractors as the U.S.S.R. at the beginning of the 1960s. While American farmers were never short of fertiliser, in 1962 Soviet state and collective farms received little more than half the corrosive chemicals they required. Commenting on the basic problems of the two agricultures, Brzezinski and Huntingdon write:

> Both Soviet ideology and the American agrarian myth have prevented the economically rational organisation of agriculture. Under the impact of the Soviet ideology, the more productive peasant plots are slowly being squeezed out by the less productive

state and collective farms. Under the impact of the agrarian myth, hundreds of thousands, if not millions, of inefficient and under-employed farmers are not encouraged to find urban employment. Yet neither ideology nor myth in itself provides a satisfactory solution. For some time to come, Soviet collectivism will have to be tempered by continual reliance on the private plots for a substantial proportion of Soviet meat and vegetables. In America, the 'independent' family farm can be maintained only by government intervention in agriculture. Pure collectivism in the Soviet Union would produce greater shortages of food, pure *laissez-faire* liberalism in American agriculture a quicker end to the small-scale family farm.

Soviet ideology has proclaimed the need to abolish the distinction between the countryside and the city by adapting factory-style organisation to the farm. The American tradition, in effect, has argued that the city should be made like the countryside by incorporating into urban culture the rural values of the independent producer and the widespread diffusion of power. Neither goal, however, has been practical. The failure of Khrushchev's early scheme for 'agro-cities' on the one hand has been matched by the frustrations of the backers of antitrust legislation on the other. Khrushchev wanted to mold agriculture in terms of a factory ideal; the rural opponents of monopoly wanted to mold industry in terms of an agrarian ideal. Paradoxically, the most efficient farms in the United States embody the industrial approach which is the ideal of Soviet agriculture. The most efficient producers in the Soviet Union, on the other hand, the peasants in their plots, embody the individual initiative and self-interest which form the ideal of American agriculture. Each system might learn something from the other. But socialist ideology and agrarian myth have made heroes out of the less productive collective farmer in the Soviet Union and the small-scale family farmer in the United States.[8]

What has been said of the agricultural sector can also be said of the industrial sector. As an American scholar has put it generally, 'we operate under conditions which may best be described as a growing buyer's market with considerable under-employment of our resources; they have a perpetual seller's market with over-full employment'.[9] In the consumer and service industries particularly, the Soviet Union has a very long way to go before it catches up with the United States; this is painfully obvious to the sympathetic visitor to Moscow or Leningrad, where the situation is presumably better than in the provinces. The Soviet press does not conceal the difficulties of moving on from its now established base of heavy industry to new achievements in the lighter industrial areas. To fulfil and over-fulfil their quotas, factories often sacrifice quality before quantity, and an article in *Pravda* telling of 28,000 complaints concerning a certain brand of refrigerator is not untypical. On the other hand production of consumer goods rose faster than that of capital goods for the first time in 1968. This, and the fact that 75 per cent of Soviet production by the end of that year was from factories which had adopted the profit ideas associated with the name of Professor Liberman, could mean that the Soviet people will soon be enjoying the rosy future which they so richly deserve.[10] A comment made by Lynn Turgeon in 1963 might then appear even more appropriate. Turgeon wrote:

> Soviet consumers are today benefiting from the nonconsumption of an earlier generation just as it is undoubtedly also true that the high American level of living today is partly the result of our ancestors' nonconsumption in the last century. There would thus seem to be a common denominator between our age of the 'Robber Barons' and their 'Stalinist Era'.[11]

The distance which Soviet industry still has to travel can readily be indicated. According to a Soviet source, at the beginning of the 1960s the U.S.S.R. was producing less than 40 per cent of the electrical energy, just under 45 per cent of the oil and just under 85 per cent of the steel produced by the U.S.A.[12] At the same time the United States made more than 8 million motor vehicles to the Soviet Union's half a million or so, about $6\frac{1}{2}$ million television sets to about 2 million, and $3\frac{3}{4}$ million refrigerators to not many more than $\frac{3}{4}$ million.[13] Total freight traffic in America was about double that of Russia's, and more varied, only 40 per cent of the former's going by rail as opposed to about 90 per cent of the latter's.[14]

Not only keeping its lead over the Soviet economy, the American sailed buoyantly through the 1960s between recession and over-rapid inflation possibly to extend it. However, this was achieved at the cost of extending limitations on capitalism. After the Truman years had been particularly bothered by industrial unrest, there was a tendency to introduce annual wage agreements and minimum wage laws. The government heated or cooled the economy whenever it was deemed necessary, and generally extended the area of its activity and control.

To a considerable degree the expansion of government interest in the economy was the result of America's involvement in wars – Korea, Vietnam and the Cold War. This continuing circumstance marked a convergence towards the command and control associated with the Soviet Union. An American observer has noted that 'Under wartime conditions our economy takes on more of the features of normal Soviet economic life, and the consequence is that our managers adopt more of the normal practices of Soviet management'.[15] Thus in Washington as well as Moscow the influence-peddler or *tolkach* plays a key part in oiling the machinery, sometimes by greasing palms. According to David Granick, bureaucracy has become a feature more marked in American than in Soviet industry.[16] Further weight can perhaps be added to the convergence argument by the fact that both economies experience difficulties internationally. All is not well by any means either with the U.S.S.R.'s 'common market', Comecon, or with the U.S.A.'s GATT and NAFTA. Ever since the Bretton Woods discussions the international monetary system has been a source of concern to the United States, and commercial and fiscal problems have by no means been absent from eastern and central Europe. Neither super-power is strong enough to control completely the economic situation within its sphere of influence.

If economic convergence between the two is in progress, the Soviet Union is finding it as difficult to make use of the profit motive and consumer demand as the United States is finding it difficult to admit planning and controls. Similarly, the super-powers cannot easily incorporate into their ideologies and myths the social developments which have been brought about by their tremendous economic development. Although American society is highly urbanised and complex, most members of it have a view of life that is rural and simple. This results in the terrible problem of the city slums, which can only be cured by a reinterpretation and enlargement of traditional American concepts of good neighbourliness. Just as their forefathers co-operated in housebuilding and harvesting, so they must be prepared to work together to see that everybody in their huge community has a decent home and standard of living. As for the Soviet Union, it is faced by the awkwardness of quite widely divergent groups emerging within a society composed officially of two nonantagonistic classes, the workers and the peasants, plus the stratum of the intelligentsia. Although inheritance laws have become less stringent in the 1960s,[17] to call the Soviet Union's 'new class' a bourgeoisie would nevertheless be incorrect, for like its Tsarist predecessor the professional stratum is dependent for its prosperity on the patronage of the state rather than on its own resources. As before, too, this stratum is separated from both workers and peasants by a considerable gap which produces tensions which are difficult to solve solely by exhortation. Moreover the comparatively new process of large-scale urbanisation presents a great problem of adjustment to peasants becoming workers. At the same time party ideologists find it no simple problem to accommodate such changes in the broad framework of Marxism.

If we are to talk of convergence in the social sense, one of the most pressing topics of conversation is the formation of one nation out of many. The American has been formed mostly by immigrants of many different origins, the new Soviet man by the fusion of nationalities, brought together initially by imperial expansion. Difficulties of identity have confronted citizens of both societies, although they have been less serious for white Protestants in the U.S.A. and for Great Russians in the U.S.S.R. It will certainly be many years before both melting-pots come off the boil, and all citizens of the two powers feel confident of their own full citizenship and lose all suspicion of that of their fellows. At the present time this seems most seriously applicable to black Americans, although not all Soviet citizens would agree with such a judgement. The stability of both societies is not helped by their continued high rate of internal migration.

We must now turn to consider one of the forces usually making for social cohesion, that of education. The comparative educational position of the two in the 1950s has been considered by N. De Witt,[18] who takes as a hypothetical base figure of 100 the number of six- or seven-year-olds in the late 1940s, about 2,900,000 in the U.S.A. and 4,300,000 in the U.S.S.R., and then goes on to give the following percentages:

U.S.A.		U.S.S.R.
99	Complete elementary schooling	98
85	Enter high (upper secondary)	55
57	Graduate from (complete schools) general secondary education	30
23	Enter institutions of higher education	10
13	Graduate from higher education	7

By the end of the 1960s the gaps in secondary and higher education have without doubt closed considerably, but such numerical convergence cannot conceal some differences between the super-powers regarding the ends of education and the means of achieving them. For example, although some of the reforms introduced by Khrushchev to reduce the separation between school and life and to promote the equality of mental and physical labour have now been withdrawn, the basic polytechnical idea of Russian education is still quite powerful. This reflects the teaching of Marx and Lenin, but also carries on a tradition stretching back at least to the beginning of the eighteenth century. If it is true, as an American educationalist has written, that 'No society has ever committed itself so unreservedly in words to the mastery and development of mathematics and the natural sciences',[19] this commitment was made more than two hundred and fifty years ago by the polytechnical Peter the Great. In America, Progressivism as a movement may be dead, but several of its tenets necessarily live on after it, because several of the circumstances which brought it into being still exist. A long tradition persists in the U.S.A. as well as in the U.S.S.R., in other words, and perhaps the differences between their educational systems are not as great as might first appear.

This argument can be developed if attention is turned to one of the charges frequently made against Soviet education, that it makes a top priority of 'totalitarian brainwashing'. This has been best dismissed by Nigel Grant, who writes:

> The educational system of any country has to be examined in its context; it is one thing to object to Communism, or Catholicism, or 'Americanism', but another to object to the fact that the schools of various countries propagate Marxism, Catholic doctrine, or the American Way of Life. It is hard to see how they could do anything else. There is little point in condemning a chisel for not being a screwdriver.[20]

A footnote to these sensible remarks might be that criticisms of the 'brainwashing' aspects of Soviet education usually come from citizens of the U.S.A., where in public schools young students regularly pledge their allegiance to the flag of the United States of America and to the republic for which it stands, and where the following 'traditions' of Lawrence High School, Kansas, are not untypical, a Lion being a student at that school:

> A patriotic Lion sings 'The Star-Spangled Banner' before the start of every 'A' team ball game.

A patriotic Lion salutes and respects the flag of the U.S. with a true sincerity and respect.[21]

The similarities between the ethical codes propagated in American schools and youth organisations and the rules of organisations for Soviet children are quite marked; these reflect the common problem of the mass education of students from differing nationalities and cultures. Moreover, parallels may be found in American education to current Soviet problems, such as the improvement of teaching standards in towns other than Leningrad and Moscow and in rural areas; the supply of more technicians and fewer technologists; and the threat to the principle of equal opportunity for all posed by the difficulty just mentioned and by the tendency for the children of white-collar workers to take better advantage of educational opportunities than the children of blue-collar workers. Of course, although such parallels can be detected, differences of degree are also to be noted: the greater seriousness of the 'blackboard jungle' in American cities; the staggering remoteness and backwardness of some Soviet rural areas.

So far, in consideration of cultural activity in general, emphasis has been placed on the development of prose fiction. Other aspects of literature have been neglected, as have the graphic and plastic arts. Moreover such extremely important themes as religion and folklore have been barely mentioned. Such omissions have been made simply because I have not felt competent to deal with them, although I am confident that illuminating comparative examinations could be made between, for example, the social significance of sectarian movements in the two communities, their folk attitudes towards the land and animals. Arriving in the present historical period, we are confronted with a problem of a different kind, the decline of literary culture and the rise of an electronic culture based on such devices as radio, television and the cinema. Already making an important appearance in the age of the proletarian revolution, the new media threaten the extinction of the old in the 1960s according to some observers. Here too I do not presume to say anything beyond the claim that useful studies could be made of, say, the manner in which the film epic has been developed by Eisenstein, Griffith and their successors. Both the decline of the old culture and the rise of the new, however, are relative; in absolute terms there are many more literate people in the world than there were thirty years ago, and the demand for books, including works of prose fiction, has never been higher; a large part of cultural experience has always been non-literary, veneration of the icon and oral tradition, to take examples from two of the themes that have been neglected. Pausing only to add the point that one of the more vigorous manifestations of the new culture has adopted the comparative approach to the super two in the shape of the Beatles' song, *Back in the U.S.S.R.*, we return to the former focus of our attention, prose fiction.

Even in this narrower, more traditional area we are faced by problems such as that of selection; which are its best representatives from the last three decades? Avoiding many of the popular works of our own time as we have avoided most bestsellers of earlier periods, we cannot adhere to our former principle of considering only those works which have stood the tests of time and of critical appraisal. We are compelled to look at books which may be deeply involved in the temporary obsessions of the war and post-war periods. Regarding the first, at least the tentative argument may be put forward that the Second World War was too enormous an experience for it to be captured successfully in imaginative writing. Possibly documentary radio and film supplanted the role of the First World War novelists and poets. Nevertheless the U.S.A. produced such varied attempts as Norman Mailer's *The Naked and the Dead*, an episodic novel in the Dos Passos tradition, and Joseph Heller's cynical satire, *Catch-22* [22] (whose hero Yossarian appears to have received the enterprising adaptability of the land of his fathers, Armenia, directly rather than by way of his nearly anagrammatic fellow-countryman, William Saroyan). From the U.S.S.R. came such war novels as Konstantin Simonov's *The Living and the Dead*, of which a comparison with Mailer's book might fruitfully be taken beyond the title, and Leonid Leonov's *The Russian Forest*. Its publishers have said of Leonov's work that it is 'a symbol of the national life'; that, 'embodied in the idea ot self-perpetuation, it becomes a criterion of the Soviet man's moral purity, his patriotism and heroic stature at a calamitous time in his country's history'. The war, apparently, could not destroy the earnest spirit of socialist realism; understandably enough, in the U.S.S.R. it was certainly looked upon as a subject too serious for humorous treatment.

Post-war novels celebrated in the West have often been anti-establishment, whether American or Soviet. However, Kerouac's beatniks, Salinger's rebel teenagers and Burroughs's junkies do not have much in common with Pasternak's Zhivago or Solzhenitsyn's Ivan Denisovich, who seem very dated in comparison with the drop-outs from affluent America.[23] But who of these will last as the dust already gathers on the literary sensations of just a few years ago? How many people now read Vladimir Dudintsev's *Not by Bread Alone* or James Gould Cozzens's *By Love Possessed*, and at what level of appreciation?

Not only literary phases pass, so do political. At the end of the period of their emergence, after years of difficulty in adjustment to each other's world power, the super-powers were perhaps moving towards an accommodation. In his inaugural address at the beginning of 1969, President Nixon declared:

> After a period of confrontation, we are entering an era of negotiation. Let all nations know that during this Administration our lines of communication will be open. We seek an open world – open to ideas, open to the exchange of goods and people, a world in which no people, great or small, will live in angry isolation.
>
> We cannot expect to make everyone our friend, but we can try to make no one our enemy. Those who would be our adversaries, let us invite to a peaceful competition – not in conquering territory or extending dominion, but in enriching the life of man.

While President Nixon wanted future generations to say of his that they helped 'make the world safe for mankind', he made no explicit attempt to fit his universalism to that of Woodrow Wilson. More concerned for ideological consistency, the Soviet leaders approached rapprochement with a more explicit acknowledgement of their predecessors' aspirations. They recalled that Lenin had spoken of the 'peaceful development of the revolution' as they pursued their policy of coexistence, and made frequent reference to Lenin's more general observation that

> Marx did not tie either his own hands or those of future leaders of the socialist revolution with regard to the forms, methods and means of the revolution, realising perfectly well what a mass of new problems would then arise, how the entire situation would change in the course of the revolution, how frequently and how much it would change in the course of the revolution.

8 Conclusion?

The present is the future becoming the past. Studies of past forecasts of the future have shown how the present has been projected forwards; studies of past analyses of the past have shown how the present has been read backwards. Our view of the contemporary world, then, is being stamped on our current interpretations of both the future and the past. Objectivity can be clutched at by the historian only if he is aware of such limitations on him. As far as the influence of time is concerned, he needs to have a sense of historical direction, to have a feeling for the manner in which the world is progressing, where it is going and where it has come from.[1] In this endeavour, he might gain some encouragement from the still relevant remarks of Sir Charles Webster made in 1923 to the effect that

> The comparative method is exceedingly valuable to historians and above all to those concerned with the difficult task of surveying impartially contemporary history. Whatever view is held of the value of history as a means of understanding the present, it at least enables us to obtain a standpoint and a perspective which can be obtained in no other way. In this strange and momentous age when new and unknown sources of energy are moulding a world before our eyes so violently that civilisation is threatened with destruction, it may be that we can find in the past some fixed points on which to take our bearings. If we are careful to remember continually the immense changes between our own day and that of a hundred years ago, and to avoid the hypnotic influence which the history of great events, in which their country has shared, exercises on some individuals, we can, I think, obtain some help in the solution of the immense problems with which we are to-day confronted.[2]

Aiming at objectivity, the historian must be conscious not only of the limitations imposed upon him by time but also of those deriving from place, from national, regional or class prejudice. The most certain weapon against this category of limitation might be the universal, co-operative history. For his part the individual can only strive to conquer his narrowness of outlook by attempting to consider the world from the point of view of others, including those anti-pathetic to him. A salutary exercise here is the study of foreign societies, which can be tackled as a comparative history of place as well as of time. As Christopher Hill has observed of such an exercise, 'applied with discretion, the comparative method is a useful tool for the historian, the nearest he can get to a laboratory test. This,' continues Hill, 'is yet another argument against the narrow parochialism which afflicts the teaching of history in too many schools and universities, and which still leads us to think of English history as something unique and God-given.'[3] To some extent, what Hill says of English historians can be said of historians of other nationalities. In the United States and the Soviet Union, however, a wider awareness is apparent among students of the subject. This reflects the responsibilities of super-power. Historians of other nationalities can at the same time surmount their ethnocentricity and assist their American and Soviet colleagues by contributing to their comparative history.

Of course, the objectivity of an approach to the drama of history is beset by a third difficulty beyond time and place, that of action. On this point, Aristotle noted that

It is necessary, then, just as in other imitative arts there is one imitation of one thing, that the plot, being an imitation of an action, should be concerned with one thing and that a whole, and that the parts of the action should be put together that if one part is shifted or taken away the whole is deranged and disjoined, for what makes no perceptible difference by its presence or absence is no part of the whole.[4]

Pursuing such a principle of unity in the imitation of the past that is their art, the slaves of Clio, consciously or unconsciously, adopt an ideology. As far as historians from the super-powers are concerned, many of them would have no difficulty in agreeing with J. H. Plumb about 'the one certain judgment of value that can be made about history, and that is *the idea of progress*.'[5] While they both take the idea of progress as their fundamental unifying principle, the Soviet historians look upon it as following Marxist laws, the American as something less defined. Yet however wide these differences of view-point, both groups of historians would have to agree that progress has shown itself in the Western world during the last three centuries or so in the following manner: from small to huge population; from an agricultural to an industrial economy; from a simplified rural society with a moving frontier to the complex class arrangements of an urban society with a fixed frontier; from absolute monarchical government to constitutional democracy; from international relations involving nations and empires to those dominated by super-powers; from illiteracy to at least universal elementary education; and from a culture based on religion to one essentially secular. The varieties of the American and Soviet experience of such progress are the basis for their comparative history.

British historians can have a special part to play in this study since much of the progress outlined above took place first in their own country, which to many observers, including Marx, has therefore appeared to present a model of that process. Moreover they are citizens of a nation whose days of imperial greatness are over, and can therefore look at the powers who have usurped their primacy with a certain disinterest as well as with some envy. They also have the advantage of intimate knowledge of the language and cultural heritage of one of the super-powers, and a long tradition of close contact with the other. However, the basic purpose of this book has not been to show that British historians should be well equipped for the comparative study of the U.S.A. and the U.S.S.R. Nor has it been to argue that such a study is an interesting academic diversion. Rather, to get back to the implications of the remarks of Webster and Hill, it can make a vital contribution to an understanding of the super-powers, to their mutual benefit.

Bold assertions such as these would best be supported by an exposition more detailed and profound than that set out in the preceding chapters. Yet they have attempted to construct a framework for a comparative history, and if they do nothing more than encourage somebody else to produce a better framework, they will have served their purpose. Certainly, whatever its weaknesses, a structure of some kind will always be as necessary for this study as for other historical investigations.

To summarise and conclude, we begin with the observation that both powers originated as frontier offshoots of western European civilisation. Russia evolved into the modern age, while America was born into it. The Russian frontier was for a long time landlocked, starting at the Muscovite centre and then radiating outwards, while the American frontier was first to be found at the edge of the Atlantic Ocean and then moved westwards. Thus, already by the end of the seventeenth century, the fundamental influences on the super two's progress into modernity had been decided. Preoccupied by the struggle for security, and cut off from the leading areas of European civilisation, the Russian state was geared primarily for war, and was extremely suspicious of possible sources of subversion, both foreign and domestic. These traits remained firmly fixed as Russia moved to the Baltic and Black seas and into the thick of eighteenth-century European affairs, and they were reinforced by her experiences during the French revolutionary and Napoleonic periods. So Russia attempted in theory to remain aloof from Europe down to the end of the nineteenth century, while in fact she became more inextricably connected with its states' system, economy and culture. Meanwhile, although fragmented along the Atlantic seaboard, American society was essentially secure from indigenous enemies by the end of the seventeenth century, and she was protected from foreign foes by Great Britain. Achieving their independence, the United States soon adopted the federal organisation implied by their past and encouraged by the relative immunity guaranteed them by the Atlantic. Still to a considerable extent dependent on Europe economically, culturally and strategically, the civilisation of the New World nurtured feelings of apartness similar to those at Europe's other extremity. Pushing its frontier relentlessly across the continent and, in a sense, into the Pacific and Latin American areas, exuberantly leapfrogging the European powers which had first experienced the process of modernisation, the U.S.A. proved to its own complete satisfaction the superiority of its democracy and constitution, of the ideology expressed in the Declaration of Independence and the Gettysburg Address.

At the beginning of the twentieth century America was potentially the greatest power in the world, and she demonstrated this during the First World War, even though she soon returned to a preoccupation with the problems of her own hemisphere. By this time the enlarged but ramshackle Russian Empire had paid the supreme penalty for its reluctance to adjust to the rapid pace of modernisation, and one of the most backward states in Europe had exchanged the most outworn ideology for the most advanced, declaring its firm intention of building a great new order. But the bricks of the old order, even some of its buildings, presented great difficulties for internal reconstruction, and a most painful period of adjustment ensued. Historic suspicion of the West was made more intense by the Communist antipathy to world capitalism, and traditional Russophobia in the West assumed a new and vigorous guise as hatred of Bolshevism. The bureaucratic-military central government of Tsarist times was replaced by one not completely dissimilar to it, although differing in its aims and personnel.

With the arrival of the Second World War, American and Soviet might emerged from the labours of the New Deal and first five-year plans to crush fascism, and to propagandise the capitalist and socialist views of democracy first enunciated by Wilson and Lenin. Capitalism and socialism both prospered in various parts of the world, in a manner conditioned by local tradition but under the protection of the super-powers. Each system drew on the experience of the other, while both lost few opportunities to declare their mutual antipathy. Somehow the world managed to survive the potentially explosive rivalry, which extended into space at a time when terrestrial developments were clearly demonstrating that there were other forces in the world besides those of the super two.

In conclusion, the hope must be expressed that peaceful coexistence will continue, and that the super-powers will learn more from each other's experience, grafting on to their own civilisation compatible practices of alien origin. In such a manner they will be better equipped to make their indispensable contribution to further human progress. The rise of China and Japan, the emergence of the rest of Asia and of Africa, the development of Europe are other vital parts of this progress, and they may in time assume even greater importance than they already possess. Moreover the speed of change has accelerated so much that the next thirty years may well contain as many surprises as the last three hundred. Nevertheless it is impossible to conceive of the world existing in the year 2000 without the United States or the Soviet Union.[6] And so, for the time being at least, useful employment may be found in working for their coexistence, which aim, I have argued, can be pursued through an examination of their pasts as well as through prediction of their futures. Certainly, if the super-powers do not continue to coexist, there appears to be a strong probability that a less tentative conclusion may ensue, both to their history and to human history in general. On the other hand, if they move beyond coexistence towards convergence, the study of their emergence will be no less relevant; after all, to know where societies are going, it is necessary to know where they have come from.

Notes

Chapter 1

1. From the preface to M. D. Kurmacheva, 'Krest'ianskaia voina 1773–1775gg. v srednem Povolzh'e', unpublished dissertation (Moscow, 1965).
2. From the summary in English of Y. L. Besmertny, 'The Present and Study of the Middle Ages', *Voprosy istorii*, no. 12 (Moscow, 1967). For a translation of the article, see *Soviet Studies in History*, VII (1968–9).
3. For Dr Pole's article, see *Journal of American Studies*, I, 1 (Cambridge, 1967).
4. The word 'whig' is used here in something like the sense of the definition given by Herbert Butterfield in *The Whig Interpretation of History* (London, 1951). In his stimulating essay, Butterfield discusses the tendency in many historians 'to praise revolutions provided they have been successful, to emphasise certain principles of progress in the past and to produce a story which is the ratification if not the glorification of the present'.
5. This and subsequent quotations from Chauncy D. Harris are taken from articles by him reprinted in Alex Inkeles and Kent Geiger, *Soviet Society: A Book of Readings* (London, 1961) pp. 5–12.

Chapter 2

1. R. R. Palmer, *The Age of the Democratic Revolution*, 2 vols (Princeton, 1959, 1964).
2. Quoted by J. C. Miller in *Triumph of Freedom, 1775–1783* (Boston, 1948) p. 586.
3. *Sbornik imperatorskogo russkogo istoricheskogo obshchestva*, XXXIII (St Petersburg, 1867) pp. 293–4. For Grimm's remarks, see p. 9 above.

Chapter 3

1. *Hansard*, 3rd ser., XXXI, pp. 615–16.
2. See I. C. Nichols, 'The Russian Ukaze and the Monroe Doctrine: A Reevaluation', *Pacific Historical Review*, XXXVI (1967).
3. R. W. Emerson, *Works* (Edinburgh, 1906) p. 949.

Chapter 4

1. M. T. Florinsky, *Russia: A History and an Interpretation* (New York, 1953) II 924–5.
2. Ibid., p. 939.

3. L. A. Cremin, *The Transformation of the School: Progressivism in American Education, 1876–1957* (New York, 1964) pp. 13–14.
4. Ibid., pp. 24–5.
5. G. Steiner, *Tolstoy or Dostoevsky* (Harmondsworth, 1967) p. 35.
6. Ibid., p. 38.

Chapter 5

1. G. Barraclough, *An Introduction to Contemporary History* (Harmondsworth, 1967) p. 20.
2. P. I. Lyashchenko, *History of the National Economy of Russia to the 1917 Revolution*, trans. L. M. Herman (New York, 1949) p. 642.
3. R. Portal, 'The Industrialisation of Russia', in *The Cambridge Economic History of Europe* (Cambridge, 1966) vi 860.
4. Quoted in S. E. Morison and H. S. Commager, *The Growth of the American Republic*, 4th ed. (New York, 1950) ii 180–1.
5. P. Miliukov, *Outlines of Russian Culture*, trans. V. Ughet and E. Davis (New York, 1960) ii 61–2.
6. See W. E. Leuchtenburg, 'Progressivism and Imperialism: The Progressive Movement and American Foreign Policy, 1898–1916', *Mississippi Valley Historical Review*, xxxix (1952–3) 483–504. For criticisms of Leuchtenburg's argument, see B. J. Bernstein and F. A. Leib, 'Progressive Republican Senators and American Imperialism, 1896–1916', *Mid-America*, l (1968).

Chapter 6

1. L. S. Feuer, 'Travelers to the Soviet Union 1917–1932: The Formation of a Component of New Deal Ideology', *American Quarterly*, xiv (summer 1962).
2. The comparison that can be drawn between the revolutionary ages of the eighteenth and twentieth centuries has been noticed by other historians. See, for example, the remark by A. J. Mayer in his *Politics and Diplomacy of Peacemaking: Containment and Counterrevolution at Versailles, 1918–1919* (New York, 1967) p. viii: 'My conception of the age of the Russian Revolution owes much to Robert Palmer's treatment of an earlier age.'
3. Morison and Commager, *The Growth of the American Republic*, ii 630.
4. A. Samsonov *et al.* (eds), *A Short History of the U.S.S.R.* (Moscow, 1965) ii 179.
5. Quoted from review of Yu. Zhukov, *Lyudi 30-kh godov*, in *The Times Literary Supplement* (2 Nov. 1967) 1026.
6. Feuer, in *American Quarterly*, xiv 148.
7. Ibid., pp. 141–2. Feuer is referring to A. Nevins and F. E. Hill, *Ford: Expansion and Challenge, 1915–1933* (New York, 1957) p. 682.
8. Cremin, *The Transformation of the School*, pp. 274–6.

Chapter 7

1. See, for example, G. Alperovitz, *Atomic Diplomacy: Hiroshima and Potsdam* (London, 1965).

2. See K. Tidmarsh, 'Can Russia Ever Turn to Capitalist West?', *The Times* (6 Oct. 1967); V. Petrov, 'The Nazi–Soviet Pact', *Problems of Communism* (Jan.–Feb. 1968); G. M. Walker (ed. and intro.), *Pearl Harbor: Roosevelt and the Coming of the War* (Boston, 1965).

3. Tavares de Sá, *The Play within the Play: The Inside Story of the U.N.* (New York, 1966), quoted in C. C. O'Brien, *The United Nations: Sacred Drama* (London, 1968).

4. By A. de Riencourt in *The Coming Caesars* (London, 1957). For a less fanciful argument, see General David M. Shoup, 'The New American Militarism', *Atlantic Monthly* (Apr. 1969).

5. See Z. Brzezinski and S. P. Huntingdon, *Political Power: U.S.A./U.S.S.R.* (New York, 1964) chap. 8, 'Civil Power in Political Crisis: Zhukov and MacArthur'.

6. Quoted in *The Times* (6 Nov. 1968).

7. J. F. Kantner, 'Basic Demographic Comparisons between the U.S.S.R. and the United States', in Inkeles and Geiger, *Soviet Society*, pp. 15–28.

8. Brzezinski and Huntingdon, *Political Power*, pp. 317–18.

9. L. Turgeon, *The Contrasting Economies: A Study of Modern Economic Systems* (Boston, 1963) p. 10.

10. M. Connock, 'Too Much, Too Soon', *Financial Times* (8 Jan. 1969).

11. Turgeon, *The Contrasting Economies*, p. 46. V. T. Bill, in *The Forgotten Class* (New York, 1959) pp. 15–16, suggests that there were Russian equivalents to the American 'Robber Barons' in the nineteenth century.

12. Yu. N. Pokataev *et al.* (eds), *SSHA proigrivaiut ekonomicheskoe sorevnovanie* (Moscow, 1961) p. 59.

13. From the table prepared by David Williams in Brzezinski and Huntingdon, *Political Power*, p. 440.

14. E. W. Williams, Jr, 'Some Aspects of the Structure and Growth of Soviet Transportation', in Joint Economic Committee, U.S. Congress, *Comparisons of the United States and Soviet Economies*, 4 parts (Washington, D.C., 1959–60) pp. 179, 187.

15. J. S. Berliner, 'Managerial Incentives and Decisionmaking: A Comparison of the United States and the Soviet Union', ibid., pp. 375–6.

16. D. Granick, 'Soviet–American Management Comparisons', ibid., p. 146. Granick published many of his observations in *The Red Executive: A Study of the Organization Man in Russian Industry* (New York, 1954).

17. See, for example, E. L. Johnson, 'Matrimonial Property in Soviet Law', in *International and Comparative Law Quarterly*, xvi (London, 1967).

18. N. De Witt, *Education and Professional Employment in the U.S.S.R.* (Washington, D.C., 1961) p. 37.

19 G. Counts, quoted by N. Grant in *Soviet Education* (Harmondsworth, 1964) p. 38.

20. Ibid., p. 151.

21. This is not meant as disparagement of Lawrence High School, where my wife spent some happy months as a student. But more generally, see the informed opinion of C. C. O'Brien that the 'American educational system is more affected by censorship and indoctrination than the standard rhetoric contrasting the open educational system of the West with the closed one of

the East would suggest': *Irish Times* (17 Mar. 1969). Objectively, however, American education is freer or less unfree than Soviet. Similarly, the treatment given to American protesters contrasts sufficiently with that given to Soviet dissidents to indicate that American life as a whole is freer or less unfree than Soviet. This is not to say that Russian governments are intrinsically more severe than American, or that socialist societies necessarily require more repression than capitalist. Here, as elsewhere, differences between the U.S.A. and the U.S.S.R. are largely explained by differences in historical development.

22. *Catch-22*'s attack on bureaucracy would certainly be applicable to some aspects of Soviet as well as of American life. See the suggestive article by B. Way, 'Formal Experiment and Social Discontent: Joseph Heller's *Catch-22*', *Journal of American Studies*, II 2 (Cambridge, 1968).

23. But this may be a false juxtaposition. A Soviet writer who would bear comparison with at least Salinger is V. Aksyonov, author of *A Starry Ticket* and *It's Time, My Friend, It's Time*.

Chapter 8

1. Here, as in chapter 1, the argument is similar to that of E. H. Carr in *What is History?* (London 1961).

2. C. Webster, *The Congress of Vienna 1814–1815 and the Conference of Paris 1919: A comparison of their Organisation and Results*, Historical Association Leaflet No. 56 (1923) p. 2.

3. C. Hill, in Introduction to T. Aston (ed.), *Crisis in Europe, 1560–1660* (London, 1965), p. 3.

4. From A. H. Gilbert, *Literary Criticism: Plato to Dryden* (Detroit, 1962) p. 81.

5. J. H. Plumb, 'The Historian's Dilemma', in J. H. Plumb (ed.), *Crisis in the Humanities* (Harmondsworth, 1964) p. 34. As indicated in Chapter 1 above (pp. 16–18), American historians would be less unanimously committed to the idea of progress, thus reflecting the freer intellectual environment in which they work and, possibly, indicating some doubt about the part to be played in world affairs by the U.S.A., in a manner similar to that in which, broadly speaking, belief in the idea of progress was abandoned by British historians after the First World War. Generally, much profit could be extracted from a comparative study of American and Soviet historians as well as of the histories of the U.S.A. and the U.S.S.R.

6. In what they call a surprise-free projection. H. Kahn and A. J. Wiener, in *The Year 2000* (New York, 1967) p. 23, expect the decline in the power of the U.S.A. and the U.S.S.R. by the end of the century to be no more than relative. On p. 265 they write: 'there are likely to be ten major powers dominating international affairs during the last third of the twentieth century: two of them "super" (United States and Soviet Union), five of them "large" (Japan, West Germany, France, China, and the United Kingdom), and three of them "intermediate" (India, Italy, and Canada).'

Select Bibliography

General

M. T. Florinsky, *Russia: A History and an Interpretation*, 2 vols (New York, 1953).

S. E. Morison and H. S. Commager, *The Growth of the American Republic*, 4th ed., 2 vols (New York, 1950).

V. N. Ponomarev, *et al.* (eds), *Istoriia SSSR s drevneishih vremen do nashih dnei*, 12 vols (Moscow, 1967–).

G. N. Sevost'ianov *et al.* (eds), *Ocherki novoi i noveishei istorii SSHA*, 2 vols (Moscow, 1960).

Others

W. H. G. Armytage, *The Rise of the Technocrats: A Social History* (London, 1965).

A. M. Babey, *Americans in Russia, 1776–1917: A Study of the American Travelers in Russia* (New York, 1938).

T. A. Bailey, *America Faces Russia: Russian–American Relations from Early Times to Our Day* (Ithaca, N.Y., 1950).

N. N. Bolkhovitinov, *Stanovlenie russko-amerikanskih otnoshenii, 1775–1815* (Moscow, 1966).

D. Brewster, *East–West Passage: A Study in Literary Relationships* (London, 1954).

Z. Brzezinski and S. P. Huntington, *Political Power: U.S.A./U.S.S.R.* (New York, 1964)

J. P. Cole, *A Geography of the U.S.S.R.* (Harmondsworth, 1967).

L. A. Cremin, *The Transformation of the School: Progressivism in American Education, 1876–1957* (New York, 1964).

F. R. Dulles, *The Road to Teheran: The Story of Russia and America, 1781–1943* (Princeton, 1944).

P. G. Filene (ed.), *American Views of Soviet Russia* (Homewood, Ill., 1968).

J. G. Fletcher, *Europe's Two Frontiers* (London, 1930).

N. Grant, *Soviet Education* (Harmondsworth, 1964).

D. Hecht, *Russian Radicals Look to America, 1825–1894* (Cambridge, Mass., 1947).

J. C. Hildt, *Early Diplomatic Negotiations of the United States with Russia* (Baltimore, 1906).

P. Hollander (ed.), *American and Soviet Society: A Reader in Comparative Sociology and Perception* (Englewood Cliffs, N.J., 1969).

E. Hölzle, *Die Revolution der zweigeteilten Welt: Eine Geschichte der Machte, 1905-1929* (München, 1963).

——, *Geschichte der zweigeteilten Welt: Amerika und Russland* (München, 1961).

——, *Russland und Amerika: Aufbruch und Begegnung zweier Weltmächte* (München, 1953).

A. Inkeles and K. Geiger, *Soviet Society: A Book of Readings* (London, 1961).

Joint Economic Committee, U.S. Congress, *Comparison of the United States and Soviet Economies*, 4 parts (Washington, D.C., 1959-60).

M. Jones, *Big Two: Life in America and Russia* (London, 1962).

M. M. Laserson, *The American Impact on Russia, Diplomatic and Ideological, 1784-1917* (London and New York, 1950).

P. I. Lyashchenko, *History of the National Economy of Russia to the 1917 Revolution*, trans. L. M. Herman (New York, 1949).

W. H. McNeill, *The Rise of the West: A History of the Human Community* (Chicago, 1963).

C. A. Manning, *Russian Influence on Early America* (New York, 1953).

A. G. Meyer, *The Soviet Political System: An Interpretation* (New York, 1965).

D. C. North, *Growth and Welfare in the American Past: A New Economic History* (Englewood Cliffs, N.J., 1966).

Yu. N. Pokataev *et al.* (eds), *SSHA proigrivaiut ekonomicheskoe sorevnovanie* (Moscow, 1961).

H. L. Roberts, *Russia and America: Dangers and Prospects* (New York, 1956).

A. D. Sakharov, *Progress, Coexistence and Intellectual Freedom* (London, 1968).

P. A. Sorokin, *Russia and the United States*, 2nd ed. (London, 1950).

L. A. Tansky, *U.S. and U.S.S.R. Aid to Developing Countries: A Comparative Study of India, Turkey, and the U.A.R.* (New York, 1967).

A. Tarsaïdze, *Czars and Presidents: The Story of a Forgotten Friendship* (New York, 1958).

B. P. Thomas, *Russo–American Relations, 1815-1867* (Baltimore, 1930).

D. W. Treadgold, *The Great Siberian Migration* (Princeton, 1957), particularly 'Foreword: Russian and American Frontiers'.

L. Turgeon, *The Contrasting Economies: A Study of Modern Economic Systems* (Boston, 1963).

P. J. D. Wiles, *The Political Economy of Communism* (Oxford, 1962).

W. A. Williams, *American-Russian Relations, 1781-1947* (New York and Toronto, 1952).

Articles

N. N. Bolkhovitinov, 'Beginnings of the Establishment of Scientific and Cultural Relations between America and Russia', *Soviet Studies in History*, v (1966-7).

——, 'The Study of United States History in the Soviet Union', *American Historical Review*, LXXIV (1968-9).

E. D. Domar, 'Special Features of Industrialisation in Planned Economies: A Comparison between the Soviet Union and the United States', in *Second*

International Conference of Economic History, Aix-en-Provence, 1962 (The Hague, 1965).

M. Ya. Gefter and V. L. Mal'kov, 'Reply to an American Scholar', *Soviet Studies in History*, v (1966–7).

A. G. Meyer, 'U.S.S.R., Incorporated', *Slavic Review*, xx (1961).

G. P. G. Sinzheimer, 'The Economics of Russian Serfdom and the Economics of American Slavery', *Jahrbücher für Geschichte Osteuropas*, N.F., xiv (1966).

I. Weinberg, 'The Problem of the Convergence of Industrial Societies: A Critical Look at the State of the Theory', *Comparative Studies in Society and History*, xi (1969).

P. J. D. Wiles, 'Will Capitalism and Communism Spontaneously Converge?', *Encounter* (June, 1963).

Index

70 71 72 73   12 11 10 9 8 7 6 5 4 3 2 1

COLOPHON BOOKS ON POLITICAL SCIENCE

*In Preparation